Valencia

Front cover: L'Hemisfèric

Below: Plaza de la Reina

TOP 10 ATTRACTIONS

Miguelete tower Climb the distinctive belltower of the cathedral *(page 32)*

Barrio del Carmen The most fashionable part of the city, both night and day *(page 36)*

Las Fallas • A spectacular festival where sculpture meets fire *(page 89)*

Torres de Serranos A reminder of the medieval city *(page 50)*

ercado Central • A temple for good food *(page 39)*

Museo de Bellas Artes • View their first-rate art collection *(page 51)*

Lonja • A silk merchants' arket dating from the 5th century *(page 40)*

La Albufera • One of Spain's most important bird habitats *(page 69)*

Museo Nacional de Cerámica • A visual feast inside and out *(page 43)*

iutat de les Arts i les Ciències • Valencia's 21st-century rchitectural showcase, with lots to see and do *(page 56)*

A PERFECT DAY

9.00am Breakfast

Start your day in the splendidly tiled Horchateria Santa Catalina (Plaza Santa Catalina, 6). Its speciality is *horchata*, a sweet, milky drink made with tigernuts usually drunk later in the day. A better choice for breakfast is a *café con leche* with an *ensaimada* (a soft, sweet bun).

11.00am Towering view

Then make your way through the atmospheric old streets of the Barrio del Carmen to the cathedral and climb its belfry, the Miguelete, for an unbeatable panoramic view over the city's rooftops.

12 noon To the seaside

Walk up the road from the Plaza del Virgen, behind the cathedral, to the river bank near the Torres del Serrano. Cross the pedestrian bridge in front of you to get to the tram station. Take line 4 to the port and have a stroll around the quayside, redeveloped for the America's Cup.

10.00am Medieval streets and Gothic architecture

For a tour of the old part of the city, head first for the Mercado Central, a glorious art nouveau market hall where you'll see Valencia at its liveliest, and then cross the road to the graceful Gothic hall of La Lonja.

IN VALENCIA

4.00pm Futuristic architecture

Catch metro line 5 to Alameda and walk up the river bank to the extraordinary gleaming white buildings of the Ciutat de les Arts i les Ciències. Looking like something out of a sci-fi movie, the City of Arts and Sciences is modern architecture at its most striking.

10.00pm A night out

Have dinner in stylish Albacar (Sorni, 35) and follow it with a nightcap in one of the many bars in the Barrio del Carmen. This is a good place to sample the city's nightlife, but don't get there too early as the action doesn't get going properly until after midnight.

2.00pm Paella lunch

Enjoy Valencia's signature dish with a long lazy paella lunch (ordered in advance) at La Pepica, or any other restaurant on the Paseo Neptuno which backs on to the beach.

7.00pm Time for tapas

Head back to the centre and join the throngs converging on the city's tapas bars for an evening drink and snack. One of the best is Bar Pilar (Moro Zeit, 13) which has been going since 1912 and is renowned for its mussels.

CONTENTS

97

89

59

INTRODUCTION

If Valencians have a reputation in Spain for being a fortunate, rather blasé people, perhaps it isn't so surprising. Spain's third-largest city after Madrid and Barcelona, Valencia has a more privileged natural setting, a more agreeable climate and, consequently, arguably a better standard of living than either.

Founded by the Romans 2,000 years ago, it stands on a shallow scoop of a bay half-way down the Mediterranean coast. Curiously, however, the city wasn't founded on the coast but a little way inland. Valencia, it always used to be said, had its back to the sea; with its commercial and fishing port kept at an avenue's length from the city centre, so that it is possible to wander around its handsome monuments, squares and gardens without any sense of being by the seaside.

Neither does the city stand on a river – at least, not any more. It may have grown up on the right bank of the

Dual roles

Valencia is a city of over three quarters of a million people. It is both the capital of a province of the same name and of an autonomous region, the Comunidad Valenciana, which stretches from the borders of Catalonia to the southern reaches of the Costa Blanca. Both city and region are bilingual with Valencian – a softer form of Catalan – enjoying equal status with Spanish (Castilian).

Turia, which flows off the high plateau in the centre of Spain into the Mediterranean, but after a disastrous flood in 1957, the decision was taken to divert the river along an artificial channel around the outer suburbs. You can still walk along the banks of what was the Turia, but you won't be walking beside a river. Ingeniously, the redundant course has been turned into an attractive feature of a different kind: an elongated ribbon of parks and sports fields crossed by a mixture of historic and strikingly new bridges.

It might not be on the sea and no longer on a river, but Valencia still remains the hub of a prodigiously fertile plain, the *huerta*, an intricate mesh of market gardens, orange groves and rice fields. The harvest wealth from these fields has always been the foundation for Valencia's prosperity and self-confidence, and the debt is duly acknowledged. Everywhere you look in the city there are motifs of fruits, flowers and a balmy country life glorified in stone and stained glass, but above all in the brilliance of multi-coloured ceramic tiles.

Valencia Transformed

Yet for all its natural advantages, Valencia has never been well known abroad and until recently has received less than its fair share of foreign visitors. This is not for want of attractive qualities. Monuments it has aplenty – especially glorious Gothic buildings dating from its 15th-century heyday when it was one of the most prosperous mercantile cities in Europe. Museums and art galleries it has too, as well as gardens, elegant public squares and grand avenues lined with palms and massive ficus trees. All this in a compact, easily walkable city centre that was largely bypassed by tourists through ignorance rather than intent.

Not any more. Simultaneously, the world has woken up to what Valencia has to offer just as Valencia itself has been waking up to the same. The city is in the grip of a new spirit for self-improvement and self-promotion. While the run-down medieval quarter of the Barrio del Carmen is being transformed into a trendy place to spend a leisurely day's sightseeing or a night crawling between bars, one of the boldest architectural initiatives in Europe, the City of Arts and Sciences, has taken shape in the reclaimed bed of the river.

The City of Arts and Sciences, a bold initiative

Everywhere you look, Valencia is busy re-fashioning itself – laying out new avenues and metro lines and building new hotels, bridges and shopping complexes. Its port was given a facelift to receive the America's Cup *(see page 13)* and has been adapted to serve as a Formula 1 circuit.

Living the Good Life

What is really striking about contemporary Valencia is not that it is bristling with new buildings, offices and infrastructure, but that it is learning to show off and share the simple, good things its people have always enjoyed. Living the good life is turning out to be the city's most marketable commodity.

Proof of this begins in the central market (one of the biggest markets in Europe), which receives the unstoppable quantities of fresh produce that pour into the city daily from farms and fishing fleets. Valencian cuisine makes straightforward use of this abundance in a range of rice dishes, outstanding

Plaza de la Reina during Las Fallas festival

among them being Spain's national dish, paella. Invented in the *huerta* and imitated the world over, a well-prepared paella is both colourful and appetising: it looks as good as it tastes. In restaurants all over Valencia you can eat the real thing – perhaps even cooked in the traditional way over a wood fire – outdoors among friends.

Then there is the nightlife, the so-called Moon of Valencia. In such a benign climate its easy to go out late and stay out late, with or without kids in tow. The extrovert parade around well-known zones of proliferating *pubs* (in the Spanish meaning of the word – loud, stripped-down, night-time-only seat-less bars), while anyone in search of a less raunchy time can cherry-pick from among a decent range of more sedate and sophisticated bars and cafés.

As if the energetic nightlife were not enough, Valencia punctuates the year with some of Spain's most showy fiestas. In particular, the Fallas in March are not to be missed.

A riotous week of non-stop noise and commotion culminates with the burning of giant comic sculptures in narrow streets and teeming squares.

City and Country

If you tire of the urban pace, there are sandy beaches to relax on; quieter towns in the Valencian hinterland to explore; and luxuriant countryside to breathe in wherever the ever-enlarging city gives up.

Country and city are united by the brilliant Mediterranean sunlight and, in spring, the wafting scent of orange blossom, or *azahar*. It's no cliché to say that Valencia is a place where the senses are constantly being stimulated: there is rarely a moment of silence nor a corner where there isn't something worth looking at. If Valencians have a tendency towards sensuality and hedonism who can blame them, and who wouldn't want to join them for at least a while?

Hosting the America's Cup

In 2003 the world's most prestigious yachting regatta, the America's Cup, was won by a European team for the first time in 152 years. The winners were Swiss, but as the rules of the competition required them to host the next challenge in their home sea, they had to select a port in a nearby country as the venue.

Thanks to its excellent wind and wave conditions, its existing facilities and its potential for development, Valencia was selected to host the 32nd America's Cup in 2007, a decision which greatly enhanced the city's esteem and led to a frenzy of building. In preparation for the event, the port was split in two with one side dedicated to commerce and the other to leisure. The prestige and facilities that came with the America's Cup have put Valencia on the Spanish tourist map in the same league as Madrid, Barcelona and Seville.

A BRIEF HISTORY

Although, as innumerable archaeological finds attest, the uplands of eastern Spain have been continuously inhabited since the Stone Age, the city of Valencia itself is of comparatively recent origin. It was founded, as Valentia, in 138BC by the Roman consul Decimus Junius Brutus to accommodate legionnaires who had served in the victorious campaign against the Lusitanians in the west of the Iberian peninsula. He chose as a site an island in the River Turia roughly equidistant between the two important Roman cities of Tarraco (Tarragona) and Cartago Nova (Cartagena). The place was marshy and inhospitable but easily defended against attacks by local tribes of Celtiberians.

As Valentia grew and thrived, its early tents and huts were replaced by mud and stone houses protected by a wall. But all this was destroyed by Pompey in 75BC as he waged civil war against Sertorius. The settlement was abandoned for almost 50 years before being reoccupied. This time it grew more securely, acquiring a forum, baths, circus, river port and systematic water supply. When the Roman Empire began to decline, however, Valentia declined with it. Its public buildings fell into disuse and entire suburbs were depopulated.

In the 4th century, a Christian community was established around the memory of St Vincent who was tortured and martyred here in 304.

Gradually, as the Church grew in power and importance, the ecclesiastical authorities assumed the gov-

El Cid

According to legend, when El Cid died in 1099, the Moors were besieging Valencia but the sight of his body being led out of the city propped up on a horse was enough to make the attackers panic. They fled the city.

Map of the Valencian region 1640

ernance of the city. However, in the mid-6th century Valencia came under the sway of the Visigoths, former allies of Rome.

Muslim Valencia

In 711 Muslim invaders from North Africa – the Moors – defeated the Visigoths and in the following years overran Spain. There is little documentary evidence from Valencia (Balansiya at that time), but it is known that the emir of Cordoba, Abd al-Rahman, sacked the city in 778 to put down a rebellion and that his son Abd allah al-Balansi built a palace in what is now the suburb of Russafa. Islam became the dominant religion – although Christianity and Judaism were tolerated – and Arabic the language of official transactions and daily life. When the caliphate of Cordoba disintegrated in 1010, Balansiya became the capital of an independent kingdom or *taifa*.

At the end of the 11th century the Christian warrior Rodrigo Díaz de Vivar, better known as El Cid, captured

Balansiya and briefly ruled it as his own fief. Shortly after his death it was recaptured by an Arab army and was to remain a Muslim city for over 130 years.

Islam was not, however, to retain its foothold in Europe forever, and the Christian reconquerors of Spain made steady progress south. As they approached Balansiya, the city's defences were strengthened, but on 9 October 1238 the city fell to Jaime (James) I, king of Catalonia and Aragón, bringing it into the mainstream of European civilisation. Under Jaime I, Muslim possessions were shared among Christian barons and the city became the capital of a new kingdom of Valencia, under the aegis of the crown of Aragón. Valencia was granted its own *furs*: laws guaranteeing its right to self-governance with its own institutions and currency.

The Middle Ages

Although the 14th century was a traumatic time for Valencia, being punctuated by rebellion, war and the Black Death, it was also a time of growth as immigrants arrived in large numbers to work in the textile industry. By the end of the century, Valencia was entering its golden age, a period of prosperity built

Legacy of the Moors

Although the Moors ruled Valencia effectively for over four centuries, few monuments have survived from that time; but they did leave something of much more lasting significance, the *huerta*. This intensely cultivated alluvial plain, which takes over where the suburbs end, is still irrigated by an ingenious system of dams and channels created by Moorish farmers to feed the prodigiously productive orchards and market gardens. Here they cultivated the crops they had brought with them to Spain: rice, sugar cane, cotton, saffron, oranges, lemons and mulberry trees (the food plant of silkworms).

on enterprise and trade. As one of the most important ports on the Mediterranean – indeed one of the most important cities in Europe – it became the most populous city in Spain, a cosmopolitan, mercantile and financial metropolis. Its docks would be busy unloading Genoese and Venetian ships which had arrived laden with Italian fabrics, gold and slaves from Africa and which would depart replete with wool, leather, ceramics and the produce of the *huerta*. The most emblematic building surviving from this time is the silk exchange of La Lonja, looking more like a temple than a trading floor.

El Cid takes Valencia from the Moors

The flow of wealth provided for a simultaneous flowering in the arts and learning: some of the first print shops in Spain were set up and the university was founded. This was also the time of two influential Valencian writers: the poet Ausias March and Joanot Martorell, the knight-author of *Tirant lo Blanc*, a novel of chivalry praised by Cervantes as 'the best book of its kind in the world'.

Despite economic and cultural prosperity, however, social, economic, religious and political tensions were building and these exploded into revolt in 1519 when the *germanías* – brotherhoods of artisans, peasants, the petty bourgeoisie and low-ranking clergy – rose up against the nobility and took control of the city. Civil war spread across the kingdom and the revolt was put down by a repressive Spanish monarchy anxious to assert its centralising authority on the regions of a newly unified Spain.

Expulsion of the Moors

There was, however, a further crisis building as the Counter-Reformation took hold in Spain. Although many Muslims had fled Valencia when it had been reconquered, many others had stayed and continued their way of life under Christian rule, accepting nominal conversion to Christianity. The Moriscos, as they were known, made up a sizeable proportion of Valencia's population. Many continued to observe the tenets of Islam in secret, wore Muslim costume and spoke Arabic. Royal decrees issued in 1525–6 sought to prohibit these lingering vestiges of Muslim Spain but, as the nobles of Valencia were economically dependent on the craft skills and labour of the Moriscos, they protected them from the Inquisition and for decades the decrees were not effectively enforced. When, at last, the Moors were expelled from Spain by Felipe (Philip) III in 1609, Valencia is estimated to have lost almost a third of its workforce, leaving some villages

18th-century tiles

without inhabitants and depriving key industries – notably that of silk-making – of their most skilled workers.

Just over a century later, Valencia again became disastrously embroiled in national politics. The death of King Carlos III without an heir divided the country – and Europe – between supporters of the Bourbon pretender Felipe V and Archduke Charles of Austria, who arrived in Spain in 1707 to claim the crown. Valencia sided with the latter but when Charles's supporters were defeated at the Battle of Almansa on 25 April 1707, the victorious Felipe took revenge with a decree abolishing the autonomous status of Valencia as enshrined centuries before in the *furs*. Along with its independence, Valencia also lost a large measure of its regional pride. A garrison of soldiers was installed in the city and a mostly Castilian aristocracy took over its administration.

Industrialisation

The 19th century was also a turbulent time for Spain, beginning with invasion. In the aftermath of the French Revolution the country was plunged into the Peninsular War (known in Spain as the War of Independence), and Valencia was twice besieged and occupied for a year and a half by the troops of Napoleon under General Suchet. Following the departure of French forces, the liberals of Spain enjoyed a brief ascendancy before Fernando (Ferdinand) VII disembarked at Valencia, declaring the restoration of the absolutist Bourbon monarchy and ushering in a period of repression. Fernando's death sparked a crisis of succession and for seven years the country was ruled by the regent María Cristina until she was forced out of power, departing from Valencia into exile in 1840. The struggle between liberalism and conservatism, royalists and republicans, went on for the rest of the century.

Notwithstanding events in Madrid, the Valencian economy grew and matured during the 19th century. The city

La Renaixença

Spearheaded by writer Constanti Llomber and journalist Teodoro Llorente, the *Renaixença* (Renaissance) cultural movement arose in the 1870s to promote the literary worth of the Valencian language and the values of Valencian identity.

rapidly industrialised. As steam engines gradually began to power factories, increasing output, so wage-labour replaced traditional artisan activities. Silk production, introduced 1,000 years before by the Moors, declined to make way for modern industries such as metallurgy, ceramics, chemicals and furniture-making – sucking in vast numbers of immigrants from the countryside. Between 1800 and 1900 the city's population grew from 50,000 to 215,000 and in the pressure to build houses, roads and railways it was decided, in 1865, to demolish the 4.5km (3 miles) of medieval city walls, creating work for potentially rebellious redundant silk factory workers. This was also a time of renaissance for Valencian regional identity, and the Valencian language and traditions regained respectability lost in centuries of centralisation.

The Civil War

For all its economic growth, Spain began the 20th century with its political problems still unresolved. The installation of the Second Republic in 1931 brought hopes of greater democracy, land reform, and the recognition of regional identities in Spain, but opinion was fast polarising between revolution and reaction. Things came to a head on 17 July 1936 when military plotters led by General Francisco Franco launched a revolt against the elected government, thereby plunging the country into civil war. Franco's Nationalist uprising failed in large parts of the country, including Valencia, which sided with the beleaguered Republic.

For a time it seemed that either side might prevail. Early on, the Nationalist forces threatened to take Madrid, and in November 1936 the government moved to Valencia, which became the de-facto capital of Spain. The parliament was housed in the city hall and La Lonja, and the government in Benicarló Palace. As the Nationalists advanced after the fall of Catalonia, refugees poured into the city, which held out until the very end. Bombed, shelled from the sea and besieged, its fate seemed inevitable. On 30 March 1939, the day before the end of hostilities, Valencia was entered by Nationalist forces under General Aranda.

The Post-war Period

In the early years of Franco's regime, the whole of Spain suffered from shortages, hunger and economic paralysis, but Valencia, which had sided against the dictator, was also subjected to a centralising, homogenising force even more severe than that of the absolutist monarchs of old. It was deprived of political autonomy, and use of the Valencian language was prohibited. As if things weren't bad enough, in 1957 the River Turia broke its banks and caused serious flooding. The river was subsequently directed into a new, artificial course around the outside of the urban area.

Anti-Fascist demonstration in the city, 1937

VIVA LARGO CABALLERO JEFE DE GOBIERNO DEL FRENTE POPULAR

Gradually, as Spain recovered economically during the 1960s, Valencia's standard of living rose and new blocks of flats were erected and motorways built, eating up the shrinking farmland of the *huerta*.

Modern Valencia

Franco's death in 1975 made way for a transition to democracy. On 23 February 1981 new-won freedoms were threatened by a coup d'etat launched by officers of the Guardia Civil. Ultimately the coup failed, but not before General Milans del Bosch ordered his tanks down the Gran Via of Valencia to point their guns at the headquarters of the Socialist Party.

The restoration of democracy brought with it the restoration of a large measure of autonomy to Spain's regions. The use of the Valencian language was now not only permitted but encouraged: it is taught in schools and given equal status to Spanish (Castilian) in all official documents.

Devolution also brought a recovery of regional pride, and since the mid 1980s the city has been getting a face lift. The old quarter of El Carmen, for a long time seedy, has been gentrified. The bed of the River Turia has been turned into a ribbon of gardens and sports facilities. A modern metro and tramway have been laid out and the long-neglected beachfront has been treated to a broad new *paseo* (promenade) lined with palm trees. But the many new buildings have been eclipsed by the opening of the City of Arts and Sciences, an ambitious project worthy of any cultured European city.

Tourist poster, 1930

Historical Landmarks

138BC Valentia founded as colony for legionnaires who had fought against the Lusitanians.

75BC Valentia destroyed by Pompey in his civil war against Sertorius.

AD304 St Vincent the Deacon is martyred in Valentia.

711 Moorish conquest of Spain.

778 Abd al-Rahman, emir of Cordoba, attacks and sacks the city.

1010 Balansiya becomes capital of a kingdom or *taifa*.

1094 El Cid takes Balansiya. In 1102 it falls again into Muslim hands.

1238 The city is conquered by Jaime I of Aragón-Catalonia.

1262 Foundation stone of Valencia cathedral laid.

1348 Black Death.

1392 Torres de Serranos built.

1474 Valencia becomes part of the Spanish state by the marriage of Fernando II of Aragón and Isabel of Castile.

1499 La Lonja completed; university founded.

1519–22 Civil war ends in defeat of the *germanías* (brotherhoods).

1609 Explusion of Moors from Spain by Felipe III.

1702–14 War of the Spanish Succession.

1707 Felipe V wins Battle of Almansa. Valencia loses its *furs* (privileges).

1812–13 Napoleonic occupation under Suchet.

1814 Fernando VIII disembarks at Valencia.

1852 Railway line built from the city centre to the port.

1865 Demolition of city walls.

1936–9 Spanish Civil War. The government abandons Madrid for Valencia in 1936. The city surrenders the day before the war ends.

1957 River Turia causes serious flooding.

1981 General Milans del Bosch orders his tanks down the Gran Via.

1982 Valencia is granted autonomous statute.

1988 Metro comes into operation.

2004 City of Arts and Sciences completed.

2007 America's Cup held in Valencia.

2011 European Grand Prix to be held in Valencia until 2014.

WHERE TO GO

The city centre, bordered to the north by the dry bed of the River Turia, to the south by the railway station and to the east and west by broad avenues, is compact enough to walk around. Most of the major sights are contained within this area. The fine arts museum and Los Viveros gardens, however, are on the far bank of the Turia but still within easy reach of the centre on foot. To travel further afield (especially to the City of Arts and Sciences) there is an efficient bus network and a metro system which connects with a modern tramway to the beach. Another option is to hire a bike *(see page 115)* and take advantage of the city's flat terrain and network of cycle lanes.

CITY CENTRE

Whether or not you arrive by train, a good place to begin a tour of Valencia is the mainline railway station, the **Estación del Norte**. Built between 1907 and 1917 in a style inspired by Austrian art nouveau, it is far more than a mere transit terminal; this is a celebration of the agricultural abundance of Valencia. Its twin white towers are hung with bunches of sculpted oranges. Inside there are yet more oranges, this time in stained glass. In the foyer and cafeteria, meanwhile, are ceramic murals depicting the life and crops of the *huerta*, the farmland around Valencia.

Street names

Many streets and squares in Valencia have two versions of their name, in the Valencian language and in Spanish (Castilian). Also, some squares have changed their names within living memory and locals often still refer to them by their former names.

Over the road from the station is the 19th-century **Plaza de Toros**, four floors of 384 identical brick arches making a structure reminiscent of a Roman amphitheatre and with seats for 17,000 people. The bullfights here during the Fallas festival in March constitute the first of the offical bullfighting season. Next to it, in Pasaje Doctor Serra, is one of the oldest bullfighting museums in Spain, the **Museo Taurino** (Tue–Sun 10am–8pm; free).

Plaza del Ayuntamiento

From the station it is only a short walk to the triangular main square, the **Plaza del Ayuntamiento**. Laid out in the 1920s, it has had four names during its short history. During Franco's time it was known in his honour as the Plaza del Caudillo but after his death, the citizens of Valencia were quick to remove the name and the statue of their defunct leader mounted proudly on a horse.

The main building presiding over the square is the **Ayuntamiento**, the city hall (Mon–Fri 10am–1.30pm except on days of official functions; free), an ornate palace of municipal authority which is essentially two buildings in one. First came a convent-like girls' school, founded in the 19th cen-

The City's Symbol

In front of the city hall, at the base of the clock tower, is a statue of the city's coat of arms held by two naked females and surmounted by a bat. The bat (*rat penat* in Valencian, meaning 'winged rat') has been Valencia's symbol since the 13th century. In 1238, while Jaime I of Aragón was going about the business of conquering Moorish-held Valencia, a bat is supposed to have perched on his helmet. This was seen as an omen of good fortune and, ever since then, the bat has been retained as a symbol of the city.

The town hall in the Plaza del Ayuntamiento

tury by the archbishop of Valencia. To this was added a dignified civic palace distinguished by its twin domes on the corner, a clock tower and a large ceremonial balcony placed in the middle. At the tower's base stand a statue of the city's coat of arms *(see page 26)*, and four statues representing Prudence, Fortitude, Justice and Temperance. Inside the city hall there is a handsome marble staircase, ornate council chamber and reception room, and municipal museum.

Across the square is the **post office** with sculpted angels, representing the speed of modern communications, hovering over its façade. The letter boxes at ground level are in the form of snarling bronze lions' heads.

If the centre of the square between these two buildings seems a little devoid of interest except for its flower stalls, it is because it is kept as a public space for fiestas. In particular, during the Fallas festival *(see page 89)*, when the largest of the city's combustible works of art is erected here. Before and during the Fallas, the square is also used as the setting for a *mascletà*, a peculiarly Valencian tradition of letting off firecrackers in synch in broad daylight with the aim not of making pretty visual effects but of creating a deafening but – or so Valencians think – harmonious din.

Plaza de la Reina and Plaza Redonda

Continue out of the square via its apex, walking in the same direction in which you arrived, and you will join Calle San Vicente Mártir. This leads you towards the second most important square, the Plaza de la Reina. On your right you pass the Pasaje Ripalda, a shopping gallery with a glass roof. Take the alley on your left before you reach Plaza de la Reina and you will step into the charming **Plaza Redonda** (which translates into English as the oxymoronic 'Round Square'). This caprice of mid-19th-century urban development, inaccessible to cars, is known affectionately by the locals as el Clot (the Hole). Arranged around the fountain in the middle is a small ring of stalls specialising in haberdashery, ceramics and work clothes.

Plaza de la Reina

You can easily get lost exploring the maze of streets beyond the Plaza Redonda, but for now it is best to retrace your steps up the alley and continue into the **Plaza**

de la Reina (formerly known as Plaza Zaragoza). As a taster before visiting the cathedral, which lies ahead of you, it is worth visiting the **Iglesia de Santa Catalina**, impossible to miss because of its distinctive baroque belltower built on a hexagonal plan. The church proper inside is not baroque at all, but a pure and soothing Gothic. Near the entrance to the church,

The cathedral's baroque Puerta de Hierros

Valencia's two oldest *horchaterías (see page 104)* face each other across the street: **El Siglo** (founded 1836) and the more spacious **Santa Catalina**, both with tiled decorations and cold marble tables.

The Cathedral

The top side of the Plaza de la Virgen is formed by Valencia's magnificent **Catedral** (winter: Mon–Fri 10am–6pm, Sat 10am–5.30pm and Sun 2–5.30pm; summer daily 10am–6.30pm; charge), with its octagonal belltower, El Miguelete, rising above it. The foundation stone for the building was laid in 1262 on the site of a mosque, and although it was begun in the prevailing Romanesque style the majority of it is Gothic. You wouldn't think so, however, as you approach it up the square because the doorway before you, the **Puerta de Hierros**, is unrestrained baroque, the work of Konrad Rudolf, a German pupil of Bernini. Although this is the main façade, it looks cramped and uncomfortable because it had to be superimposed on a pre-existing building, with the immovable El Miguelete taking up much of the space.

To appreciate better the simplicity of the cathedral it is best to skirt round it to the right and enter by the earliest doorway, the rounded Romanesque **Puerta del Palau**, which gives on to the Plaza del Palacio del Arzobispal. This has a pleasingly understated decoration. The 14 small heads under the cornice are said to represent seven men and their wives who came from Lerida to repopulate Valencia after the Christians had reconquered it from the Moors.

Once inside the cathedral you can fully appreciate its basic Gothic structure. The nave is now of clean stone – most of the extraneous 18th-century decoration having been removed in the 1980s.

It is lit by an elegant *cimborrio*, an ocatagonal, two-

Valencia's Holy Grail

Like Turin's shroud, the purported Holy Grail in Valencia's cathedral has been the subject of a great deal of speculation. In 1960, a professor of archaeology at Zaragoza University dismantled and examined the cup and proclaimed it to be of a date prior to Jesus Christ and made in a workshop of the Near East; but there is no evidence connecting it directly to New Testament events.

According to legend it was taken from Jerusalem to Rome by Saint Peter and there used by popes to celebrate mass. When the Emperor Valerian persecuted the Church and tried to confiscate its treasures, San Lorenzo – the first deacon of the Church – dispatched the grail to Huesca, in the Pyrenean foothills, for safety, three days before being martyred for his faith. It now made its appearance in historical documents. During the Muslim conquest of the Iberian Peninsula, the grail was kept in the remote monastery of San Juan de la Peña.

In 1437 it arrived in Valencia where it has been ever since, except during the Napoleonic occupation of Spain when it was smuggled out for safe-keeping.

The cathedral's Gothic nave

storey lantern which is pierced by windows of delicate tracery, the sunlight filtered through panes of alabaster.

The altar, however, is an elaborate accumulation of Renaissance and baroque art, the altarpiece being by two artists heavily influenced by Leonardo da Vinci. One grisly point of interest behind the altar is the brown and shrivelled mummified forearm of St Vincent the Deacon, co-patron of the city, who was martyred in Valencia in 304.

Altogether more beguiling is the cathedral's most famous relic, what is claimed to be the **Holy Grail**, the cup that Jesus Christ drank out of at the Last Supper *(see page 30)*. The small, dark red agate cup, which in the 14th century was set in a gold framework studded with jewels, is on display in a gloomy chapel, formerly a chapterhouse, beneath a roof of stellar vaulting sprouting from coloured bosses.

The Chapel of the Holy Grail gives access to the **cathedral museum** (charge) which houses a few treasures, including some of the original polychrome statues, two paintings by Goya, other paintings by Juan de Juanes and a giant monstrance which is taken through the streets of Valencia during the procession of Corpus Christi.

The last thing to do before leaving the cathedral is to climb the octagonal belltower of the **Miguelete** (Micalet in Valencian; daily 10.30am–1pm and 4.30–7pm; charge), which demands the giddying ascent of a spiral staircase of more than 200 steps to a terrace over 50m (160ft) above the city streets below. The tower owes its name to having been consecrated on 29 September 1418, the feast day of the archangel St Michael, Miguelete being the affectionately diminutive form of his name.

The Miguelete

From the tower, peels rang across the city in the late Middle Ages announcing the times to open and close the city gates. The bellcote crowning the tower today is, however, a later addition.

Outside the Cathedral

Leave the cathedral by the door opposite the main entrance, the **Puerta de los Apóstoles**, a triumph of 14th-century Gothic sculpture attributed to Nicolás de Ancona. Looking behind you, you can admire the veritable crowd of Biblical characters gathered around the door, including 14 angels, 16 saints, 18 prophets and, to the sides of the door, the apostles standing on triangular pillars and sheltered by tabernacles. All these statues were originally coloured and kept repainted until at least 1522 when they began to be badly worn by the elements. The worst eroded were withdrawn in modern times and have been replaced with copies.

Outside the cathedral

Every Thursday at 12 noon this doorway becomes the setting for what is perhaps the most extraordinary court of law anywhere in the world. It is here that the **Water Tribunal** meets in public and in the open air to decide disputes between farmers over the use of irrigation water in the *huerta* around the city. The eight judges dressed in black smocks – all farmers themselves, elected by their peers – represent the different networks of water channels. Hearings are instant and oral (in Valencian): no records are taken; no appeal is possible: and no business is put off until another session. The court has met in this way weekly, with scarcely a break since 1239. When there is no debate the affair can be over while the clock is still striking midday – so get there promptly if you want to see it.

Plaza de la Virgen

The Puerta de los Apóstoles lets you out into the **Plaza de la Virgen** (built on top of the Roman forum), which is now a car-free place to mill around, feed pigeons, or sit in a pavement café and watch life go by. In the middle of the square is a fountain representing the god Triton, personifying the River Turia, surrounded by eight figures with pitchers pouring water, represening the principal irrigation channels feeding the *huerta*.

The cathedral shares this square with two other impressive buildings. Beside the Puerta de los Apóstoles is what looks almost like a lost section of the Colosseum. This is an arcaded gallery belonging to the cathedral known as **Els Balconets de la Seu**, which serves as a dais from which church dignitaries can watch processions and other events taking place in the square. The most spectcular of these events is La Ofrenda, part of the Fallas festival in March, when a huge copy of the statue of Valencia's patroness, the Virgin de los Demparados (the Virgin of the Forsaken or Helpless), is made out of bunches of flowers brought by a lengthy procession of people dressed in traditional costume.

The fountain on Plaza de la Virgen

The actual statue of the Virgin is of a more modest size and form, although obscured by the wig, rich clothes and jewels that lavishly adorn her.

The statue is kept on display above the altar in the church dedicated to her, the 17th-century **Basílica de los Desamparados** (daily 7am–2pm and 4.30–9pm; free). The first entirely baroque building to be erected in Valencia, it is connected to the cathedral's dais by a high,

enclosed bridge of Renaissance style used by members of the clergy only. The statue is poised on a swivel mechanism so that it can be brought to face the nave of the church or a small chapel intended for more intimate communion with the faithful. During Las Fallas she is honoured by a large display of flowers in the square outside the church.

Behind the church, through the arch formed by the bridge to the cathedral, is the Plaza Almoyna, site of the original Roman settlement of Valentia, off which are two lesser sights: an art gallery, the **Museo de la Ciudad** housed in the former Palacio del Marqués de Campo, and **El Almudín**, a 13th–14th-century granary which once supplied the city with wheat and is now used to house exhibitions. Down an adjacent street, Calle del Almirante, is the only piece of Moorish architecture still standing in the city, the **Baños del Almirante** (Admiral's Baths; Tue–Sat 10am–2pm and 6–8pm, Sun 10am–2pm; guided visits every half hour; charge).

The other conspicuous building on the Plaza de la Virgen,

5 ▶ set back from it slightly, is the seat of the Valencian regional government, the **Palau de la Generalitat**. It looks old enough to be a fusion of Reniassance and Gothic, but only one tower is authentic – the other is a copy added in 1952. Inside the old tower are several magnificent public rooms which, unfortunately, are not open to visitors

Another important institution is housed in an old palace on the pedestranised Calle Navellos, which leads north from the Plaza de la Virgen towards the Torres de Serranos and the river. This is the **Cortes** (Mon and Fri by appointment only, tel: 96 387 61 00; free), the regional parliament of the Comunidad Valenciana. It occupies the much-extended Palacio de Benicarló, which became the home of the Republican government in the Civil War after its exile from Madrid until the final victory of Franco's forces.

Barrio del Carmen

6 ▶ Take the street that runs beside the Palau de la Generalitat and you are on Calle Caballeros, the principal axis of Valencia's oldest and most atmospheric quarter, the **Barrio del Carmen**, an organic network of narrow, erratically twisting streets and alleys which suddenly open out into unsuspected little squares, where you can sometimes hear the silence despite being in the heart of a modern city. For decades during the 20th century, this area was left to crumble into squalid, undesirable tenement housing; chunks of plaster were regularly dislodged from its discoloured walls by the ricochets of fireworks during the Fallas fiestas. Finally, however, the city council decided to rehabilitate it, allowing the area's unique character and the buildings' surviving architectural details to be enjoyed. At night it is transformed into one of Valencia's favourite nightlife haunts.

For a taste of the Barrio del Carmen you can just walk along **Calle Caballeros**, athough this is not one of its typical streets because of the wealth of its residents. It is lined with mansions of more or less Gothic pedigree, mostly built around inner patios – which are often concealed behind street doors large enough to admit carriages when opened but forbidding enough to keep the riff-raff out when shut.

A better policy is to venture off this main street northwards. A right turn down Calle Salinas brings you to a curious example of how architecture can be adapted to new uses. A semicircular arch, the **Portal de Valldigna**, was once part of the 2-m (6½-ft) thick wall built by Valencia's Muslim rulers and later used as a point of access to the medieval Christian city. In the 17th century, two houses on either side of the street were joined together over the top of the gate.

Barrio del Carmen, a favourite place to eat

If you continue wandering in the same direction, you will come to the rectangular Plaza del Carmen, one of the oldest squares in the city, overlooked by the **Iglesia del Carmen**, founded in the 13th century and much altered since. It has a baroque façade on three levels and an angel as a weathervane. The church once formed part of a Carmelite convent, which now contains the **Museo del Carmen**; Tue–Sun 10am–8pm; free), displaying late-19th century to early-20th century Valencian art.

At the end of Calle Caballeros is the Plaza del Tossal. Here a section of the Moorish-era wall, together with a watchtower, can be seen in the **Galería del Tossal** (Tue–Sat 10am–2pm and 4.30–8.30pm, Sun 10am–3pm; charge). It is believed to be part of the al-Hanax gate, one of the city's five entrance points in the wall built between 1021 and 1061 when Valencia was capital of a Muslim kingdom.

A short walk beyond the Plaza del Tossal, down Calle de Quart, brings you to the edge of the Barrio del Carmen, marked by the **Torres de Quart**, one of the old city gates. This was built between 1441 and 1460, using Naples' Castel Nuovo as a model. When the walls fell into disuse, the gate was turned into a women's prison. The holes that can be seen in the outside walls are said to have been made by projectiles fired by the French during their siege of Valencia in 1808 and left unrepaired as a memorial to the resilience of the citizens.

Iglesia del Carmen

The Market and La Lonja

South of the Barrio del Carmen, down Calle Bolsería from Plaza del Tossal, you come to three very different buildings sharing the triangular **Plaza del Mercado**, where those deemed heretics by the Inquisition were burned at the stake.

Church of the Sts John

8 ▶ The **Iglesia de los Santos Juanes** began life as a Gothic structure, built on the site of a mosque. It was badly damaged by fires in the 16th century and had to be almost totally rebuilt during the 17th and 18th centuries. Only the nave and a large blank disc at the west end, which was to have been a rose window,

suggest the church's Gothic origins; otherwise it is a somewhat disappointing baroque. Still, the frescoes of the Apocalypse on the vaults by Antonio Palomino are worth seeing as are the statues of the Twelve Tribes of Israel, sculpted by Jacobo Bertessi.

The main façade, forming an odd juxtaposition with the other two buildings on the square, is unusual for having a terrace jutting out from its base which was used as a platform from which dignitaries could watch public spectacles. Below it are basement chambers with doors onto the street known as **les covetes de Sant Joan** (St John's caves), which used to house tiny bric-a-brac shops. At the top of the façade is a clocktower with figures of the two St Johns to whom the church is dedicated.

Mercado Central

Adjacent to the church is the antidote to a morning spent sightseeing too many historical monuments: the **Mercado Central** ◀ **9** (Mon–Sat 7.30am–2.30pm). The principal market of the city, indeed one of the biggest markets in Europe, is housed in a handsome art-nouveau building with wrought-iron vaults and a central dome. Designed for the everyday business of buying and selling, it nevertheless has delightful ornamental touches in ceramic, brick and stained glass – most notably the red and yellow stripes of Valencia's flag, the *senyera*. When it was inaugurated in 1928 by King Alfonso XIII the market had well over 1,000 stalls. Consolidation among the traders has reduced this number to around 700, which still gives the shopper plenty of choice. The best time to get here is mid-morning when it bustles with people calling out their orders in Valencian and stuffing shopping baskets and trolleys with fruits and vegetables. If you are not going out into the *huerta*, where oranges are sold by growers by the roadsides, buy them here. Some stalls also sell herbs and spices, others dried fruit and nuts, and one specialises in ostrich eggs and meat. A separate part of the market is for fish and seafood.

Outside, if you are peckish, you can get some freshly fried *churros* – like long, thin doughnuts – a popular sweet snack, or a takeaway portion of paella. A stall near the entrance sells paella pans in a range of sizes with gas rings to match, together with the necessary cooking implements.

La Lonja

Across the road from the market is Valencia's favourite building, a true temple to commerce. **La Lonja** (Tue–Sat 10am–2pm and 4.30–8.30pm, Sun 10am–3pm; charge), originally used for trading in silk and later as a general commodities exchange, is one of Europe's finest examples of civil Gothic architecture. It was modelled on a similar building in Palma de Mallorca and built between 1483 and 1498.

The exterior is lavishly decorated in carved stone with tracery, filigree, *ajimez* windows (divided into two lights by slender columns) and spiky crenellations beneath which gargoyles leap out. If you look closely at street level you can get a glimpse of the more playful side of the craftsmen respon-

Mercado Central

sible: among the figures incorporated in the stonework is one showing his naked buttocks to the observer.

The building is divided into three parts by a central tower, which contains a chapel and a prison once used for merchants who defaulted on their debts. The part to the left of the tower was occupied by two institutions: the **Consulado del Mar**, the regulatory body that oversaw maritime trade, and the **Taula de Canvis**, the city's first banking body, which was largely responsible for financing the construction of La Lonja.

Entering to the right of the tower, you step immediately into the building's most graceful space, the **Transactions Hall**, which is divided into three naves. The high ceiling is held aloft by eight gracefully spiralling columns which sprout at the top into stellar vaulting. An inscription running round the chamber reads, 'I am a famous house which took fifteen years to build. See how fine a thing commerce can be when

its words are not deceitful, when it keeps its oaths and does not practise usury. The merchant who lives in such a way will have riches and enjoy eternal life.'

Behind La Lonja is a warren of narrow streets and squares dotted with small shops. With luck you should emerge underneath the tower of the Iglesia de Santa Catalina, at the corner of the Plaza de la Virgen, ready to visit a very different part of the city centre.

Museo de Cerámica
From the bottom of Plaza de la Reina, a straight street, **Calle de la Paz**, leads towards the modern shopping zone

Interior of La Lonja, the
15th-century silk merchants' market

of the city centre. Take the second
turning on the left, Calle Marqués
de Dos Aguas, to get to Spain's
national ceramics museum, the
Museo Nacional de Cerámica
González Martí (Tue–Sat 10am–
2pm and 4–8pm; Sun 10am–2pm;
charge). This is contained within
an extraordinary building, the
Churrigueresque (an extreme
Spanish form of baroque) mansion of the Marquis of Dos Aguas:
an 18th-century extravaganza of
coloured plaster. The doorway is
particularly striking. It is a drip-
ping fantasy in alabaster designed
by Hipólito Rovira (who is said to
have gone insane later) and executed by the sculptor Ignacio Ver-
gara. Ostensibly it is a portrait of the **Virgen del Rosario**
but below it becomes a pun on the marquis' surname, Two
Waters. On either side of the door two semi-nude male figures recline lethargically, while below them water representing the two rivers of Valencia, the Turia and Júcar,
flows from twin pitchers. Around the figures runs a volup-
tuous mass of vegetation.

Beyond the portal, the museum doesn't disappoint. The
name is happily misleading as the collection covers much
more than ceramics. It is an eclectic delight of all things old
and dazzling – even if you can't warm to pottery and porcelain, you are likely to find something to fascinate you. To

The Museo Nacional de Cerámica González Martí

begin with there are the rooms of the mansion itself, with their spiralling gold columns hung with grapes, cherubs, and pink plaster cornices. They form the backdrop to everything on display. The most striking single exhibit, perhaps, is the marquis' Cinderella-style formal **Carriage of the Nymphs**, another Rovira/Vergara over-indulgence in excessive ornamentation. Other things to be seen include canopied beds and various items of furniture, a collection of Ex-Libris bookplates, old posters, photographs, books, sketches, engravings, caricatures, jewellery, silver and ephemera galore to do with celebrated Valencians.

The ceramics museum proper has some 5,000 pieces beginning with prehistoric, Greek and Roman specimens, passing through Oriental pieces, and ending with creations by Picasso. The core of it was amassed by Manuel Gonzalez Marti, discoverer of potteries that flourished in the Middle Ages near Valencia. The outstanding treasures of the museum are medieval pieces made in ceramic-making towns near Valencia – Paterna, Manises and at the Royal Factory in Alcora – which are executed in greens, blacks and blues, often with metallic sheens. Among the more unusual pieces are 15th- and 16th-century examples of a technique associated with Paterna known as *socarrat* (between toasted and burnt). These tiles, which were designed to be placed between the beams on the ceiling, depict animals, flowers, ships, geometric patterns in spontaneous lines and rough shapes of red or black. The most popular exhibit in the museum is a complete traditional **19th-century Valencian kitchen** richly decked out in ceramic tiles with panels depicting food and animals.

To see a more mundane use of ceramic decoration, continue down the street (it becomes Poeta Querol after the museum) until you come to the corner formed by the Teatro Principal. Look up left at the upper storeys of the neo-baroque 1935 triangular building of the **Banco de Valencia** building which forms a rounded corner between two streets. Above the penultimate balcony are two floors adorned with brightly coloured tilework against a contrasting red background.

The University and El Patriarca

The streets opposite the ceramics museum lead to two venerable Valencian institutions, the university and El Patriarca. The neo-classical university was begun in the 15th century, although it is largely the result of later work.

Next to the university is the Real Colegio de Corpus Cristi, commonly known as the **Colegio del Patriarca** (daily 11am–1pm; charge), in honour of its founder, the 16th-century archbishop and viceroy of Valencia, and Patriarch of Antioch, St John de Ribera (1532–1611). Ribera was a leading spirit of the Counter-Reformation, the repressive principles of

Inside the ceramics museum

which he applied in the seminary he founded. The focal point of the complex is a two-storey Renaissance patio composed of a double gallery of arches supported by 56 marble columns shipped in from Genoa. The statue in the middle of the courtyard depicts the archbishop himself, sculpted by local artist Mariano Benlliure.

To one side of the patio is a **church** whose walls and ceilings are entirely covered with richly coloured frescoes by Bartolomé Matarana. The 9.30am service (Tue–Sun) is in Gregorian chant. Above the altar you will normally see a beautiful version of the Last Supper by Francisco Ribalta, but during Friday morning mass (at 10.25) this is theatrically lowered to reveal a painting of the crucifixion by an anonymous 15th-century German artist hidden beneath.

There are various works of art scattered around the Patriarca, including some fine Brussels tapestries. But several rooms are specifically dedicated to displaying an important collection of paintings by Spanish and foreign masters, including El Greco, Juan de Juanes, Caravaggio, Sariñena, Ribalta, Van der Weyden and Morales.

The philosopher

In the patio of the university stands a statue of Valencian-born Juan Luis Vives (1492–1540), also known as Ludovicus. This brilliant philosopher and humanist spent most of his life outside Spain because of persecution due to his Jewish roots. In England he tutored Princess Mary (later Mary I) and took up a post at Oxford, where he formed close friendships with Thomas More and Erasmus.

ALONG THE RIVER TURIA

It's not every city that can turn its river into a pedestrian urban freeway, but that is what Valencia has effectively done. After serious floods in 1957, the Turia was diverted through the outskirts to the

Taking a promenade by the River Turia

south leaving its dry bed still flowing through the urban area in a large and strategic arc west to east. The bold decision was then taken to make the former course of the river into a ribbon of green for recreational use and the celebration of the arts, and it now serves as an elongated sports and cultural resource available to all, its amenities joined up by pedestrian and cycle routes.

For over 6km (4 miles), from the Puente Nou d'Octubre to the Puente de Astilleros, the riverbed is a procession of gardens, sports fields and playgrounds, all planted with a variety of trees, either native to the region or adapted to the climate, notable among them pines, palms, carobs and olives. Between these two crossing points are a further 17 bridges, seven of them expressly built as part of the riverbed rehabilitation project. If you want to walk the whole length of the river, begin at Nou d'Octubre station on metro line 3 in the suburb of Mislata (there are several buses that go there too).

The Upper Turia

This river of gardens begins upstream in the west with the **Parque de Cabecera** (or **Capçalera**). Next to the park is the extraordinary **Bioparc**, an extensive zoo which recreates different African habitats.

The park is divided into several ecosystems: savannah, equatorial African forest, African wetlands and that of Madagascar. The African savannah includes an acacia forest and is inhabited by zebras, impalas, giraffes and rhinoceros. Big rocky formations recreate a typical African landscape, and lions rest on top of rocks overlooking the zebras and antelopes. There is also a palm forest inspired by those found in Kenya, and a stand of baobabs where a herd of African elephants can be seen drinking at the lake (summer: daily 9.30am–sunset; winter: 10am–6pm; charge).

Next to this, on Calle Valencia, a continuation of the Passeig de Petchina (which runs along the southern riverbank), is the **Museo de Historia de Valencia** (Tue–Sat 10am–2pm 4.30–8.30pm, Sun 10am–3pm; charge), housed in an atmospheric 19th-century water cistern. The exhibits tell the story of the city from its foundation by the Romans to the present day. Every section is equipped with a 'time machine', consisting of a life-size screen on which actors portray scenes from history in the language of your choice.

Follow the south bank of the river and on the other side of the Puente de Ademuz you'll find the **Museu Valencià d'Historia Natural** (Natural History Museum; Sat–Sun 10am–2pm; charge). Behind this is the **Jardín Botánico** (Tue–Sun 10am–6pm; closes 2 hours later in summer; charge), a university botanic garden created on the present site – which was then outside the city walls – in 1802. It is planted with 4,500 species organised into 20 collections, including plants useful to humans, a tropical greenhouse, water plants, carnivorous plants, native Valencian species, woodlands and

Lily pond in the Jardin Botánico

palms. Its most original feature is the Umbraculo, a pergola built of brick and iron.

A little further down the southern river bank, on the corner of Calle Guillem de Castro, is the **Instituto Valenciano de Arte Moderno** (IVAM; Tue–Sun 10am–8pm; guided visits by appointment; charge), which is considered one of the top modern art galleries in Spain. The permanent collection concentrates on Julio Gonzalez, acclaimed as the father of 20th-century Spanish sculpture. Its eight galleries include one in which remains of the medieval city wall can be seen.

If you prefer art at the opposite end of the chronological spectrum, have a look a the prehistory museum next to the IVAM, the **Museu de Prehistòria i de les Cultures de València** (Tue–Sun 10am–8pm; free), in which you can see undeciphered engravings made by prehistoric people living in the hills of Valencia.

Round the bend in the river, just after Puente de San José, is a museum of art of a different kind, the **Casa Museo de José Benlliure** (Tue–Sat 10am–2pm and 4.30–8pm; Sun 10am–3pm; charge). This is the former home of the prominent Valencian painter José Benlliure who died in 1937. National galleries and private collectors have taken the most interesting works. There is a pretty garden with Valencian ceramics to wander round.

The next monument you come to, still on the same bank of the river, is the **Torres de Serranos** (Tue–Sat 10am–2pm and 4.30–8.30pm, Sun 10am–3pm; charge). One of the few remaining bits of Valencia's medieval city walls – and more glamorous than the Torres de Quart *(see page 38)* – this gateway was built in the 14th century using one of the doors of Poblet monastery in Catalonia as a model and combines defensive and decorative features. Its two towers are topped by battlements as if ready for war, but the central panel over the gateway is embellished with delicate Gothic tracery, giving a clue that this is more triumphal arch than defensive installation. Its structure was left exposed at the back to prevent the towers being used against the citizenry. From the Plaza de los Fueros behind you can see its various

Torres de Serranos

chambers – which have cross-ribbed vaults – once used as a jail for miscreant nobles. Four gargoyles protrude from this rear wall.

Across the next bridge, the Pont de Fusta, is a railway station, once used for a quaint system of narrow-gauge railways but now serving the high-tech tram which departs for the beach. Down this next stretch of the northern bank of the river are two monumental buildings and two gardens. At the end of Puente de la Trinidad is the **Real Monasterio de la Trinidad** (only open for mass), a working convent inhabited by a closed order of nuns. The monastery door is pure Flamboyant Gothic.

Museo de Bellas Artes

Next to this is the **Museo de Bellas Artes** (Museum of Fine Arts; Tue–Sun 10am–8pm; free) housed in a 17th-century seminary. This might not compete in size with the large galleries of Madrid and Barcelona but it has an important collection nonetheless, focusing on painting of the Gothic period. You enter via an octagonal vestibule covered by a blue cupola and ascend two floors of galleries. Upstairs, the most outstanding pieces are 'primitive' Valencian painting of the 14th and 15th centuries, represented by a series of huge golden altarpieces painted in tempera and later, under Flemish influence, in oils by artists such as Jacomart, Miguel Alcanyis, Maestro de Bonastre and Pere Nic-

Valencian artists

One part of the Fine Arts Museum of particular interest presents the work of three little-known Valencian artists of the 19th and 20th centuries who were inspired by the sea, the colours of the *huerta* and the light cast by the Mediterranean sunshine: Ignacio Pinazo, Antonio Muñoz Degrain and, above all, the Impressionist Joaquín Sorolla.

Inside the Museo de Bellas Artes

olau. Other outstanding works include Hieronymus Bosch's *Triptych of the Passion*, showing the tormenting of Christ, and Velázquez's self-portrait. There are also works by El Greco, Van Dyck, Murillo, Ribalta and the local Renaissance painter, Juan de Juanes. There are six paintings by Goya here, although none of them is exceptional.

Los Viveros and Beyond

The Museo de Bellas Artes stands at the corner of the city's largest garden, the Jardines del Real, better known locally as **Los Viveros** (The Nurseries; daily 8am–sunset; free). The garden has a wide variety of different spaces within it connected by broad *paseos*. There are fountains, pergolas, a restaurant often used for weddings, lawns, ornately decorated benches, bronze and marble sculptures galore and a lake with ducks. Here and there are intriguing bits of historic architecture salvaged from demolition sites: a baroque doorway, a pink and grey marble fountain from a monastery, and sample houses from the Valencian *huerta*. The garden also includes the **Museo de Ciencias Naturales** (Natural Sciences Museum; Tue–Sat 10am–3pm and 4.30–8pm, Sun 10am–8pm; charge).

Near Los Viveros, a few steps away from the riverbed, are more gardens, this time protected from the rush and noise of the city by a wall. The **Jardines de Monforte** were creat- ed in the 19th century by Juan Bautista Romero, a wealthy Valencian landowner, and designed by the architect of the bullring (*see page 26*). They are Italian in inspiration and neo-classical in style, with hedges closely trimmed into geometric forms, a long shady arbour, trickling fountains and a scattering of sculptures and marble statues, creating many intimate spaces.

From the corner of Los Viveros, the next kilometre of the left or north bank of the river becomes the Paseo de la Alameda, a broad avenue. Diagonally across the river from Los Viveros are two churches which would be worth seeing but are hard to visit: the **Iglesia del Temple** (open for mass only), which, as its name suggests, owes its origins to the Knights Templar, and the **Iglesia de Santo Domingo** (group visits only by appointment 8am–2pm; tel: 96 196 30 38), which has a beautiful Gothic cloister and 15th-century chapel but is now owned by the military.

Four bridges stand close to each other here, beginning with the stark white **Puente de Calatrava**. Built

Elio's mountains

Los Viveros occupies the site of a Moorish country house, later Christian palace and royal residence which was demolished during the Peninsular War. When the war was over, rubble from the palace was swept together to form two artificial hills, Las Montañitas de Elio, named after the general who ordered their building.

'La Peineta'

The sleek, white Puente de Calatrava has been given the nickname of 'La Peineta' for its resemblance to the ornamental combs worn by women as part of the traditional Valencian costume.

of extra-tensile steel and with a span of 131m (430ft) supported by a single arch set at 70 degrees from the horizontal, it was designed by the Valencian architect Santiago Calatrava, who is also responsible for the adjacent metro station (and most of the Ciutat de les Arts i les Ciències).

On the city side of the river is the **Plaza Porta del Mar**, marking the site of the gate in the city wall that communicated with the harbour. This was the last gate to be closed at night and anyone absent-mindedly arriving late was forced to sleep in the open air across the river, giving rise to the expression 'to be left out under the moon of Valencia', meaning to be left in the lurch. These days the term Luna de Valencia (Moon of Valencia) has been expropriated to refer to the city's nightlife.

A short way further down the river is the 10-arched **Puente del Mar**, built in 1591 and one of the oldest bridges still standing. Each end is marked by broad flights of steps and the bridge itself is adorned with canopied sculptures of the Virgin Mary and St Paschal.

Continuing down the riverbed parklands, the next sight you come to, beyond the Puente de Aragón, is the **Palau de la Música**, an ultra-modern concert hall which could almost be a greenhouse for the amount of glass incorporated into its remarkable construction. The main auditorium has such excellent acoustics that the Spanish tenor Plácido Domingo is said to have remarked after his first concert here that 'El Palau is a Stradivarius'. As well as ballet, opera, classical and jazz concerts, the Palau also hosts modern art exhibitions.

The Final Stretch

Over the other side of the next bridge, Puente del Angel Custodio, a giant sculpture of Jonathan Swift's **Gulliver** lies pros-
trate in the riverbed acting as a great climbing frame and
slide for children.

The last bridge before reaching the riverbed's end at the
Ciutat de les Arts i les Ciènces is the city's longest. The
Puente del Reino marches obliquely across the river taking
a nonchalant 220m (720ft) to get from one bank to the other
and is lit by art-deco lampposts. Raised on plinths at either
end are the guardians of the bridge: four snarling pseudo-
Gothic gargoyles in bronze, human of body but with the
heads of beasts and half-unfurled wings, designed by the en-
gineer who built the bridge, Salvadór Monleón.

There is one more sight of interest on the south bank of
the river, easily overlooked, and that is the **Museo Fallero**

Palau de la Música

on the corner of Plaza Monteolivete (Tue–Sat 10am– 3pm and 4.30–8.30pm, Sun 10am–3pm; charge). The museum honours the tradition of the Fallas, the fireworks festivals held each year in March *(see page 89)*, and houses *ninots*, comic figures in papier-mâché, which have been saved by popular acclaim from the usual conflagration.

THE CITY OF ARTS AND SCIENCES

As the bed of the River Turia nears the sea, the new developments along it reach a spectacular climax in the futuristic cultural complex of the **Ciutat de les Arts i les Ciències**, the City of Arts and Sciences. This ambitious complex aims to encourage visitors to combine leisure with an exploration of the arts, sciences and nature. It consists of five stunning, futuristic buildings, four of them by Santiago Calatrava, standing in a 1.8-km (1-mile) alignment.

Palau de les Arts

Approaching from the city, the first of the buildings is a spectacular concert hall, the **Palau de les Arts Reina Sofía**, which has a 75-m- (250-ft-) high, domed roof clad in white

Visiting the City of Arts and Sciences

Except for the Oceanogràfic, it is possible to walk around the City of Arts and Sciences (www.cac.es) at your leisure and enjoy much of the architecture for free. If you want to visit all parts of it inside and out, however, you'll need to buy a combined ticket giving admission to L'Hemisfèric, the Museu de Les Ciències Príncipe Felipe and L'Oceanogràfic. A ticket can be bought from any of the ticket offices or by phoning 90 210 00 31. This is valid for one, two or three days (they don't have to be consecutive) and permits you to visit each attraction once only.

The dramatic City of Arts and Sciences

mosaic tiles. This was the last part of the complex to be completed. The building houses four separate theatres with a combined capacity of over 4,000 seats, designed to provide Valencia with a world-class stage for high-quality opera, concerts, ballet and theatre.

L'Hemisfèric

The concert hall is separated from the other buildings by a bridge, the Puente de Monteolivete, on the other side of which is a hi-tech cinema, **L'Hemisfèric**, the first part of the city to open in 1998. This eye-shaped cinema has sides like folding portcullises which open and close in imitation of a blinking eyelid. Its singular aspect has been enhanced by placing it between two symmetrical shallow rectangular ponds. Under what turns out to be an elaborate oval canopy is a sphere stuffed with high technology where banks of comfortable seats look up at a gigantic, inclined, concave screen 24m (80ft) in diameter. The Hemisfèric's main function is to project the moving images of IMAX films which exceed the limits of human binocular vision, sucking the viewer into the larger-than-life action. It is an overwhelming sensory experience which can be dizzying and disorientating. The cinema is also geared up for laser shows and as a planetarium in which more than 9,000 stars are visible.

Museu de les Ciències Príncipe Felipe

The next building is one of Spain's largest science museums, the **Museu de les Ciències Príncipe Felipe** (daily 10am–8pm, till 9pm on Sat; charge), a sloping skeletal structure of steel and glass composed of vast intersecting white arches and taut buttresses. It looks like a cross between a cathedral, a space-age aircraft hangar, and the chalky skeleton of some fossilised sea creature.

The exhibitions are arranged on four floors, although you can walk about some parts of the building, notably Calle Mayor and the terrace, both one level up from the entrance, without paying the admission fee. The contents are fairly standard science museum exhibits, covering life, the Earth, science and technology with many interactive exhibits, and in term time the place is often filled with school parties.

L'Umbracle

Opposite the science museum, across another shallow rectangular pond, is the **L'Umbracle** (daily 10am–7pm; free). This is essentially a cleverly disguised car park forming the south side of the complex and screening the rest of it from the road. The roof of the car park has been turned into a a winter garden, covered by what looks like a giant white cloche – *umbracle* means arbour or pergola – 18m (60ft) high. If L'Umbracle is the least spectacular part of the city, it is also the most peaceful and a pleasant place to stroll around when you want to get away from the crowds elsewhere. It is planted with various species of shrubs and trees native to Valencia and others selected for their adaptation to the climate. As the space has to make either an artistic or scientific contribution to the whole, there are several sculptures to admire in the shade, including *EX IT* by Yoko Ono.

L'Oceanogràfic

The final and largest part of the city is technically an aquarium but is, in reality, far more than that. **L'Oceanogràfic** (daily 10am–6pm, till 8pm on Saturdays, till midnight in summer; charge) is made up of a series of lagoons containing water varying according to salinity, temperature and depth to represent the five oceans, and various pavilions or towers illustrating different marine environments – oceans, wetlands (topped by a spherical aviary), tropical seas and the Arctic.

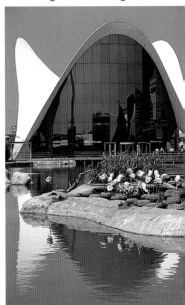

Flamingos at L'Oceanogràfic

The last of these is an appealing igloo-like dome which is agreeably cool on a hot day outside. The whole place is connected by bridges, passageways and underwater glass tunnels – one being the longest such tunnel in the world.

Although it's certainly an imaginative juxtaposition of original architecture and wildlife, it could be said that there isn't enough of the latter to do justice to the former, even if the figures sound impressive: there are 10,000 individuals of 500 different marine species floating above, below or around you or, as is more usual in aquariums, sitting in dark corners of their tanks doing nothing. The whole place is conceived on three different levels and there are also a lot of ramps, stairs and lifts to negotiate as you go down into the depths to look at each habitat. Several events are staged during the day to add interest to a visit. The highlight of these is the dolphin and killer-whale show and it is worth making a note of the time of the next show when you arrive and getting to the dolphinarium early to save a seat.

THE SEAFRONT

Although much of Valencia's historical prosperity derived from its role as Mediterranean port, until recently the city always kept its distance from – and its back to – the sea. The urban centre grew up just over 3km (2 miles) from the coast, far enough for the harbour area, El Grau, to be thought of as a distinct, unsavoury haunt of sailors, poor fishermen and lowlifes. Even today, the inhabitants of the maritime quarters – mostly proud people with strong local traditions – speak of 'going to Valencia'. In the city centre, meanwhile, there is scarcely a hint of sea nearby except in the name of Avenida del Puerto, built at the start of the 20th century, leading discreetly off towards maritime perdition.

The beach is sandy and fine for swimming

The relationship only started to change in the 1960s when new suburbs filled the void between the two parts of the city. But then came tourism, which made city planners realise that their seashore was something to develop rather than ignore. The shabby port was spruced up, a new promenade *(paseo marítimo)* built for seaside recreation, and now there are controversial plans to continue Avenida Blasco Ibañez to the beach by bulldozing part of the historic Cabanyal fishing quarter. The final step in the rehabilitation of the seafront's reputation was the awarding of the 2007 America's Cup competition to Valencia *(see page 13)*.

Until the extension of Avenida Blasco Ibañez goes ahead, there are two ways to see the sea. The most direct way is still by bus or taxi down Avenida del Puerto, a straight street running from the Plaza Zaragoza at the end of Puente de Aragón, which these days is on its way up-market. A more interesting trip is by tram from the Pont de Fusta station, across the riverbed from the Torres de Serranos; take metro line 4 in the direction of Doctor Lluch and get off at Les Arenes.

The Port

In preparation for the America's Cup, Valencia's port has been split neatly in two. The south side concerns itself with the container and passenger terminals (catering for trippers to and from Mallorca and Ibiza), while the wharves on the north side, adjacent to the beach, have been transformed into a marina and leisure complex which is pleasant to stroll around. There is also a Formula 1 circuit hosting the European Grand Prix (until 2014). Some of the more attractive parts of the old port have been retained on the side nearest the Avenida del Mar, including the handsome **Port Authority Building** with its distinctive clock tower and some warehouses in a restrained mercantile brand of art nouveau.

Fishing on the seafront

The new developments centre on a striking modern structure, the **Edificio Veles e Vents** (Sails and Winds Building; also know as the America's Cup Building), an iconic water pavilion designed by UK architect David Chipperfield. ◀ **26**

Set back from the harbour, next to the church of Santa María del Mar, is Valencia's maritime museum, housed in **Las Atarazanas** (Plaza Juan Antonio Benlliure; Tue–Sat ◀ **27** 10am–2pm and 4.30–8pm, Sun 10am–3pm; free), an ensemble of five Gothic sheds built at the end of the 16th century to serve as a workshop for boat building, an arsenal and a place to store maritime tackle. At the time of their building they stood at the head of the beach.

The Paseo de Neptuno and Paseo Marítimo

Stepping out of the side entrance of the port brings you onto Valencia's flashy esplanade, the **Paseo Marítimo**, which be- ◀ **28** gins with the pleasant **Paseo de Neptuno**. Along this little street are the front doors of a solid line of restaurants specialising in paella. Each has its back door opening onto the beach and almost all of them have glass-enclosed dining rooms and terraces. At weekends and in summer they can be very busy; at other times of the year you may well get the whole restaurant to yourself – but don't take this as an indication that the food is not good. Prices along the restaurant strip vary and three establishments trade on ancient fame: La Pepica, L'Estimat and La Marcelina.

The Paseo de Neptuno ends abruptly at the luxury spa hotel of **Las Arenas** (or Arenes), which retains two restored bright-blue classical temples (entirely rebuilt) that were once part of the old-fashioned restaurant complex that stood here.

From the corner of Les Arenas, the Paseo Marítimo becomes a 2-km (1¼-mile), palm-shaded multi-lane pedestrian motorway of dog walkers, pram pushers, joggers, ice-cream-licking toddlers and power-walking grannies. There is also a cycle track

Casa-Museo Blasco Ibáñez

along the length of it. In summer the beach beside it can be packed with sunbathers, but off-season the fine golden sand provides a pitch for impromptu games of football or frisbee. The sea, except in exceptionally bad weather, has only a light swell, and is good for swimming: despite its proximity to a commercial port, most people consider it suitably clean.

For its last stretch, the Paseo Marítimo runs along **Calle Isabel de Villena**, where, in the late 19th and early 20th centuries affluent Valencians built themselves fine holiday villas. Among these worthies was the novelist and sometime republican-leaning politician Vicente Blasco Ibáñez (1867–1928) who found inspiration from the uninterrupted views of the sea. His reconstructed house is open to the public as the **Casa-Museo Blasco Ibáñez** (Tue–Sat 10am–2pm and 4.30–8.30pm, Sun 10am–3pm; charge), containing portraits, photographs and sculptures of the writer, books and memorabilia.

The Cabanyal
A few streets back from the Paseo Marítimo is one of Valencia's best-kept secrets, the old fishing quarter of the **Cabanyal**. This was once a defiantly self-contained community where everyone knew everyone and fishermen would sit on the pave-

ments outside their houses mending their nets. You can still see signs of this spirit in a few surviving family-run corner shops and neighbourhood bars, the best of which is the Casa Montaña, which was founded in 1836 *(see page 110)*.

There are no museums or monuments of note in the Cabanyal. Instead, the charm is in the ordinary architecture, at least those examples which have survived successive attempts at modernisation. The Cabanyal grew up as a patchwork of *barracas*, typical Valencian houses with steeply pitched thatch roofs, that were aligned in long streets parallel to the beach so that fishing nets could be laid out to dry. Gradually, around the turn of the 19th and into the 20th century the *barracas* were replaced by small, low family homes which were less vulnerable to fire. Many of these were decorated by their owners on the outside in eclectic, highly idiosyncratic styles broadly inspired by *modernismo*, the Spanish version of art nouveau.

Several of the houses have façades entirely clad in colourful ceramic tiles, which reflect heat and humidity and keep the interiors cool. Others, especially near the seafront, are tastefully painted in one or two pastel shades. Everywhere there are playful details to admire: intricate ironwork ornaments, stucco motifs, a Phaoronic head on the tiles of a balcony, a frieze hinting at Moorish Spain, tulips rampant up a door jamb, gargoyles and grotesque heads peering over the street. Look for them on any of the old streets: Reina, Barraca, Padre Luis Navarro, José Benlliure or Escalante.

Almost all the old houses in the Cabanyal are low level, of human proportions; many are back-to-backs and some are so small

Easter Week

The Easter Week procession through the Cabanyal puts the rest of Valencia to shame with its ostentatious legions of participants dressed as Biblical characters, Roman soldiers and, strangely, Napoleonic grenadiers.

Villa in the *huerta*

that they have only one room upstairs and one downstairs. Anywhere else in Western Europe, the entire Cabanyal would be listed as a historic quarter and every house older than 50 years protected, but every year some little corner of it falls to the bulldozers with little attempt made to salvage the architectural treasures it contained.

AROUND THE CITY

Valencia's hinterland is easily explored by car or public transport from the city centre. You have a choice of fertile farmland, a watery nature reserve, historic ceramics-making centres or a medieval monastery.

The Huerta

If it is possible to visit Valencia without being reminded of the proximity of the sea, it isn't easy to come away ignorant of the existence of an intensely fertile agricultural plain surrounding the city. Valencians have an almost spiritual attachment to this prime piece of farmland, the *huerta*. From its produce their city originally grew wealthy; later it was relied on to help them survive through hard times; and today the *huerta* continues to fill markets and provide the raw materials for Valencia's traditional dishes and drinks.

Yet this natural resource is under threat from modernity. Theoretically, the *huerta* extends over a semicircle of land roughly bordered by the River Júcar to the south and the hills that start around Sagunt in the north. In practice, however, it is shrinking rapidly as it is encroached on by the growth of dormitory towns and the inexorable expansion of the outskirts of the metropolis.

But there is still *huerta* left and in places you can get an idea of how it must have looked in the days when agriculture was a leading industry here. At its most perfect, close to the city, the *huerta* is composed of smallholdings where not even the smallest patch of land is allowed to go to waste. The fine soil beneath the immaculate rows of artichokes, tomatoes, aubergines and flowers looks as if it has been sifted, fed and spoiled for generations, which it undoubtedly has. Given the warm climate, these plots can produce up to four crops a year if they are worked with care.

The highly cultivated *huerta*

Such high productivity, of course, depends upon water. Crucial to farming the *huerta* are the *acequias* (irrigation channels) whose use and misuse is argued over weekly by the members of the Water Tribunal *(see page 33)*. On its arrival at Valencia, the River Turia is checked by an ingenious system of dams, sluices and overflows which feeds eight principal *acequias* in proportion to the amount of land they supply. These and other less noble *acequias* crisscross the *huerta*, branching into ever smaller divisions to form a watery labyrinth of glistening channels. The original irrigation system was probably devised by the Romans, but it is the Moors who are credited with perfecting it; they came from Syria, Lebanon and Egypt where they knew all about the importance of irrigation to farming.

That the *huerta* has made fortunes for some enterprising farmers can be seen in the proud, exotic farmhouses, *alquerias*, that poke out from among the foliage. Some of them have towers and fanciful oriental touches; many have ceramic ornamentation gleaming in the sun. Much less common are *barracas*: traditional peasant houses with steeply pitched thatched roofs.

30 ▶ One corner of the *huerta*, **Alboraya**, has built its fortune by specialising in a particular crop, the *chufa* or earth almond, *Cyperus esculentus*, a brilliant green, spiky, grass-like plant which is thought to have been introduced by the Moors. When the tubers of this plant are mashed with water and sugar they become *horchata*, a sweet milky drink which is served cold in summer *(see page 104)*. The *chufas* of Valencia have their own *denominación de origen*, like wine grapes.

Lakeside fisherman

Another plant introduced to Spain by the Moors is the orange, which has since become Valencia's most famous export crop.

When the trees flower in late February to early March the sweet smell of the blossom – *azahar* – fills the air and even pervades the built-up areas. String bags of ripe oranges hung on sale by the side of the road or next to a front door are a common sight in the first few months of the year. When buying oranges, don't be put off by their often blotchy or scarred appearance. These unattractive fruit, rejected by wholesale

Barraca in La Albufera

export buyers, have plenty of juice and an intense flavour. The tastiest oranges, it is said, remain in Valencia.

La Albufera

To the south of the city, where there is even more water available, the *huerta* becomes a checkerboard of paddy fields which are sown and flooded in the spring for the rice to mature over the summer. In July and August the leaves of the crop reach full height and the whole area flushes a vivid emerald green. Over winter, after the autumn harvest, the landscape turns into a watery maze.

The rice fields converge on **La Albufera**, a freshwater lake
beside the coast which is one of the Iberian Peninsula's prime

wetlands for birds *(see below)* and easily reached from Valencia by the motorway to El Saler. The lake is fed by the River Turia and connected to the sea by three channels or *golas* which are fitted with sluice gates to control the water level. It is extremely shallow, up to only 2.5m (8ft) deep, and is gradually shrinking because of natural silting and the reclamation of land by rice farmers. In the Middle Ages the lake was 10 times its present size.

If your main interest is primarily wildlife you may want to go first to **Raco de l'Olla** (by the turn-off to El Palmar), where there is an information centre (daily 9am–2pm, Tue and Thur 4–6.30pm; tel: 96 162 73 45; free) with a glass-domed observation tower for birdwatching. On the other hand if you are more interested in food, the village of **El Palmar** is the authentic place to eat paella and *all i pebre* (eels cooked with garlic and pepper). El Palmar is also the departure point for boat trips around parts of the lake.

If you are feeling adventurous you can try to negotiate the tracks that lead around the edges of the rice fields and along irrigation channels south from El Palmar to the low hill of **La Muntanyeta de Sants** and, eventually, the N332 main road.

La Albufera is separated from the sea by a strip of sand dunes and Mediterranean woodland, 10km (6 miles) long

Birds of La Albufera

Well over 300 species of bird have been recorded in La Albufera, a figure which includes vagrants making a one-off appearance. With patience and binoculars you are usually sure to see herons (night, squacco and purple), egrets (cattle and little), ducks, waders, terns and gulls. Shy species like the bittern make good use of the lake's reed beds and marshy islands, *matas*, to hide in. The bird population spills over into the neighbouring rice fields in search of food.

Nature-watch boat trip on the lake

and 1km (½ mile) wide, called the **Dehesa** which is fringed with sandy beaches, making it popular with tourists. When the beach-lovers have gone home it is a good place to take an evening stroll.

Ceramics Towns

Manises, next to Valencia's airport, has been synonymous with ceramics since the Moors introduced the craft. The **Museo de Cerámica de Manises** (Tue–Sat 10am–1pm and 4–7pm, Sun 11am–2pm; free) has a permanent exhibition of 2,500 pieces dating from the 14th century to the present day. It's worth taking a stroll around the old town to browse in the ceramics shops and to see some beautiful tiled façades and colourful door jambs.

There are more ceramics in **Tavernes Blanques**, a short way north of the city, where the Lladró company has its factory and the **Centro Cultural y Museo Lladró** (Mon–Fri

9.30–5pm, Sat 9.30am–1pm by prior appointment; tel: 90 021 10 10; free). Visitors see the whole process from design to the kiln, together with an exhibtion of current and past products. The Lladró brothers' art collection – including works by El Greco, Sorolla, Zubarán Ribera and other Spanish artists – is on display in a separate hall.

El Puig Monastery

About 15km (9 miles) north of Valencia is the Mercedarian **Real Monasterio del Puig de Santa Maria** (Tue–Sat 10am–noon and 4–5pm; visit by guided tour only, beginning on the hour; charge). In 1237, on the eve of the conquest of Valencia by the forces of King Jaime I, a statue of the Virgin Mary was found on a hill on this spot. A church was built to house the statue, which was adopted as the patroness of the new Christian kingdom. In 1588 the church gave way to

El Puig Monastery

the monastery, a forbidding rectangular building with four stout corner towers. The guided visit takes you through two cloisters and into the refectory, chapel, hall and other rooms where there are numerous works of art.

In one wing is the **Museo de la Imprenta y de la Obra Gráfica** (Museum of Printing and Graphic Arts), which has a facsimile of what is thought to be the first book printed in Spain: *Les Obres o Trobes en Lahors a la Verge Maria*, printed in Valencia in 1474.

EXCURSIONS

Many varied but little-known places are within reach of the city of Valencia, especially if you have hired a car – although most can be reached with public transport. The easiest to get to are on the coast, or at least on the coastal plain. The nearest of them are still in Valencia province, but rewarding one- or two-day excursions can be made northwards to the Costa del Azahar, the coast of Castellón province, and south towards Alicante and the Costa Blanca. There is also good scenery and much of interest in the hills inland. Below are the nearest and most worthwhile destinations for a day out.

Via Augusta

Once Spain had been brought fully under Roman control, the Emperor Augustus (27BC–AD14) ordered a road to be built down the east coast, linking the Pyrenees and Cádiz. Named the Via Augusta after the emperor, it extended 1,500km (930 miles) and was the longest Roman road in the Iberian Peninsula. Although it was primarily intended to enable troop movements, it also facilitated trade. Its route runs through Sagunt to Valencia where it passes through the Plaza de la Reina in the centre of the city.

Sagunt

In 219BC, Saguntum, a Roman outpost on the Via Augusta whose foundation long predates Valencia, was sacked by the Carthaginian general Hannibal, an attack which was to spark the Second Punic War and lead to the subjugation of Spain by Rome. Among other monuments, the Romans built a theatre on the hillside above the present-day town of **Sagunt** (30km/18½ miles north of Valencia by road or rail), exploiting a natural hollow for its acoustic effects.

In 1896 this theatre was the first building in Spain to be declared a national monument. In the 1980s the decision was taken to rehabilitate it for contemporary performances of drama and music, but the restoration work made controversial use of new materials and techniques and not everyone has been happy with the result.

On the crest of the hill above is a sprawling **castle**, which from the 5th century BC was the site of the Iberian settlement of Arse. Over the centuries it was added to by successive civilisations. Almost 1km (½ mile) in length, it is divided into seven plazas or divisions. There are beautiful views from it over the town and the sea. (The castle and Roman theatre are open Tue–Sat 10am–2pm and 4–6pm, till 8pm in summer, Sun 10am–2pm; charge.)

Sagunt viewed from the castle

Below the theatre and castle, the core of the **old town** is medieval, set around the porticoed main square. The most atmospheric part is the old Jewish quarter, which is laid out in irregular narrow streets and passageways.

The Knights Templar castle at Peñíscola

Peñíscola

In the extreme north of Castellón province is the old fortified town of **Peñíscola** (140km/87 miles north of Valencia
on the A7 motorway), built on a rocky promontory into the
sea. Its castle, the **Castell del Papa Luna**, erected on the
foundations of a Moorish fortress, is mainly the work of the
Knights Templar and their cross can be seen carved above
the door. It later became the residence of the papal pretender
Pedro de Luna, cardinal of Aragón, who was elected Pope
Benedict XIII during the Great Schism that split the Christian Church at the end of the 14th century. He retired here
after he had been deposed and died a nonagenarian in 1423
still proclaiming his right to the papacy. The castle was used
as a location for the film *El Cid*. Beneath the castle walls is
a delightful labyrinth of steep, narrow cobbled streets lined
with white houses, enclosed by massive ramparts and entered
by two gates.

Palacio Ducal in Gandía

To the north of the old town is an immensely long, straight sandy beach stretching to the next resort of Benicarló. There is also a smaller curve of beach to the south, next to the harbour.

Gandía

The Duchy of **Gandía** (65km/40 miles south of Valencia by the A7 motorway) was bought by one Rodrigo Borja in 1485. As Pope Alexander VI he founded the clan known better by the Italian spelling of its name, Borgia. He himself is remembered for his scandalous private life, but his illegitimate son, Cesare, and daughter, Lucrezia, have become definitions of debauchery. The family's reputation was redeemed by Alexander's great-grandson, who was born in Gandía in 1510 and canonised in 1671 as St Francis Borgia. Following the death of his wife, he turned his back on the pleasures of the world, joined the Society of Jesus (the Jesuits) and devoted himself to spreading the ideas of the Counter-Reformation.

For all his saintly work he remained a nobleman and his birthplace, the **Palacio Ducal** (Duke's Palace; Mon–Sat 10am–2pm and 4–6pm in winter, Mon–Sat 10am–2pm and 5–7pm in summer, Sun 10am–2pm; visited by guided tour only; charge), is an opulent building inside, even if no hint of this is given by the simple Gothic courtyard you enter by. The interior decoration, with its painted ceilings and gilded doorways, reaches a zenith in the baroque Golden Gallery, commissioned by the 10th duke of Gandía to celebrate his ancestor's canonisation. One room on the tour has a concentric circular tiled floor made in Manises *(see page 71)* representing the four elements of earth, air, fire and water. Gandía has some beautiful sandy beaches and is known for its typical dish, *fideuà*, a kind of paella made with vermicelli instead of rice *(see page 101)*.

Xàtiva (Játiva)

You can follow the Borgia line backwards by going inland from Gandía to **Xàtiva** (60km/37 miles southwest of Valencia), the birthplace of the two popes who founded the clan. The Phoenecians are thought to have first settled the site. In the 11th century, Europe's first paper was made in Xàtiva by the Moors out of rice and straw. A huge ribbon of a **castle** (Tue–Sun 10am–7pm, closes 6pm in winter; charge), with 30 towers, once the most important fortress under the Crown of Aragón, runs along the ridge above the town. On the way up to the castle are two very old chapels: the 13th-century **San Feliu** (St Felix; Tue–Sun 10am–1pm and 3–6pm in winter; 10am–1pm and 4–7pm in summer), which has a

◀ 36

The Upside-down King

Xàtiva was a prosperous place until, as part of the kingdom of Valencia, it backed the losing side in the War of the Spanish Succession, that of Archduke Charles of Austria. Retribution followed the Battle of Almansa in 1707, when the victor, Felipe V, burnt down the town and renamed it San Felipe. In the 19th century, the city fathers reclaimed the old Moorish name and exacted their revenge by hanging Felipe's portrait upside down in the municipal museum – and that's the way it has remained.

Romanesque doorway, pink marble columns and paintings from the 14th and 15th centuries, and **San José** (Tue–Sun 11am–1pm), which has a viewpoint outside it.

Among the sights in the narrow streets and small squares of the old part of the town are a former hospital with a Plateresque façade (opposite the 16th-century collegiate church), and a medieval fountain in Plaça de la Trinidad. The **municipal museum** (Tue–Sun 10am–2.30pm and 4–6pm; charge), meanwhile, has an unusual royal portrait in its collection *(see box on page 77)*.

Denia and Jávea (Xàbia)

The two closest resorts of the Costa Blanca to Valencia are Denia (100km/62 miles south by the A7 motorway) and Jávea (10km/6 miles further), separated by the humpbacked hill and nature reserve of Mount Montgó (753m/2,470ft). They are very different in character from each other and between them offer a range of beaches.

The bigger and busier of the two is **Denia**, which was founded as a Greek colony and named after the goddess Diana. For a while in the Middle Ages it was the capital of a Moorish kingdom and the oldest parts of its **castle** date from that time. North of the harbour, past the old fishermen's quarter, is the long, wide sandy beach of Las Marinas; to the south is the more discreet and rocky Las Rotas, which has some good snorkelling. In the first two weeks of July Denia holds its Toros a la Mar festival, a bull-run up to the water's edge.

Jávea, over the hill, is in two parts. Its town centre is

Raisin' the roof

Many of the older houses in the countryside surrounding Jávea have an unusual feature testifying to the local land use: a *riu-rau*, an arched stone porch where grapes were hung to dry into raisins in the circulating air.

Beach bar in Jávea

perched on a hill a short way inland, on the site of an Iberian settlement. Many of the buildings lining the streets – including the town hall and cinema – are made from the local characteristic *tosca* sandstone. The 16th-century church of **San Bartolomé** is an imposing piece of work as it was fortified to serve its congregation as a refuge in times of invasion. Over the door are machicolations through which missiles would be dropped on to attackers.

Most buildings around the port and main beach, which are overlooked by a line of ruined 17th- and 18th-century windmills, are modern but relatively low-level as a result of council policy to keep Jávea from being dominated by the high-rise apartment blocks seen in other resorts.

The rest of Jávea's shoreline is rocky. Pirates and smugglers once took advantage of the hiding places afforded by the cliffs, caves and inlets between the lighthouse at Cape San Antonio and Granadella Cove.

WHAT TO DO

SHOPPING

Valencia is a pleasant city in which to shop. If it lacks the specialist or chic retail outlets of Madrid and Barcelona, at least it isn't overwhelming in its variety. It has a good balance between small, old-fashioned family-run shops and ultra-modern shopping centres. Plus it has the advantage that you can get around most of the shops on foot, without straying out of the city centre.

Although manufacturing has declined in favour of service industries, Valencia still offers a few traditional specialities that make good souvenirs: ceramics is its main craft, but locally made leather and wooden goods (guitars, castanets, pipes), fans and, most practical of all, paella pans are all available.

Where to Look

The modern shopping streets of Valencia lie roughly within an area bounded by the busy streets of Colón, San Vicente Mártir, Játiva and Calle de la Paz. They include Don Juan de Austria, Barcas, Roger de Lauria and Correos. All these streets are within an easy walk of the Plaza del Ayuntamiento. The shopping continues down Jorge Juan and around the Mercado de Colón and along the Gran Vía Marqués del Turia. Traditional craft shops are around the cathedral area and behind the Lonja.

Department Stores and Shopping Centres

A good one-stop shop for just about anything is **El Corte Inglés** department store, which has eight branches that all stay open, unusually, at lunchtime. The main ones are Pintor Sorolla 26 (on the corner of Jardines del Parterre, at the end of Calle de la Paz) for fashion, and Calle Colón 27 for everything else, including books and recorded music, and it has a good basement supermarket selling Spanish delicacies.

The closest shopping centres to the city centre, all filled with national and international chain stores, are **Nuevo Centro** (which has a branch of Corte Inglés), across the riverbed, and **El Saler**, opposite the City of Arts and Sciences.

Markets and Street Markets

The **Mercado Central** *(see page 39)* is a tourist attraction in itself, and the art-nouveau **Mercado de Colón** (no longer a working market) is also a delight. But for a real feel of the city visit a neighbourhood market such as the **Mercado Ruzafa** or the **Mercado del Cabanyal**, near the seafront.

There is a street market every day of the week in one part of the city or another, with stalls selling cut-price clothes and household items. The most important are in **Calle Convento Jerusalen** on Tuesdays, **El Cabanyal** (around the market) on Thursdays and **Benicalap** on Saturdays. Sundays is flea-market *(rastro)* day around the **Plaza Redonda** where a bit of everything, including books, plants and animals, is on display, and in **Mestalla** next to the football stadium, where mainly secondhand goods are on sale. Also on Sunday mornings, stamp and coin collectors converge on **La Lonja**.

Fashion

The best places to look for designer labels and jewellery are calles Colón, Sorní, Cirilo Amorós, Jorge Juan and Ensanche. The most expensive shops are in this area. **Loewe** has a shop at Marqués de Dos Aguas 7 (for women) and Poeta Querol 7 (for men); next-door to the latter is **Louis Vuitton**. The Spanish fashion designer **Adolfo Dominguez** has a shop at Hernán Cortés 30. Nearby, in Calle Colón, are two Spanish chains with more affordable prices, **Zara** and **Mango**.

Ceramics and Other Crafts

The best place to shop for ceramics is Manises *(see page 71)*, but there are a number of good shops in the centre of the city where you'll find a range of household items and ornaments. Try, for instance, **Artesanía Cerámica Campayo** (Calle Cordellats 2) or **Artesanía Colla Monlleó** (Plaza Redonda 12). Also in Plaza Redonda, **Chez Ramón** sells hand-made ceramics and wrought-iron lamps. Nearby, at Plaza Milagro de Mocaoret 5, a tiny square through an arch from Plaza de la Reina, is **Yuste** which sells ceramics, crafts and custom-made items. **Lladró**, the world-famous porcelain manufacturer *(see page 71)* has a shop at Poeta Querol 9, facing the ceramics museum.

Traditional Spanish fans – very practical for hot, summer days – have been made near Valencia since the 15th century. You will find a wide variety of fans at a range of prices in

Pottery stall in Plaza de la Reina

Rosalen (Calle Sant Vicent Mártir 19) and **Bisuteria Nela** (Calle San Vicente 2, near Plaza de la Virgen). However, the best place to shop for them is, without doubt, **Abanicos Carbonell** (Castellón 21, tel: 96 341 53 95; www.abanicos carbonell.com), a family business which has been going since 1810 and is run by a fourth-generation master fan-maker who will show you his collection of 18th- to 21st-century fans on request. Some fans are less functional accessories than *objets d'art*, each one the work of perhaps 20 different craftsmen.

Other crafts shops are **Huerta de San Vicente** (San Vicente 41), which sells craftwork from Andalucía and the rest of Spain; and, for jewellery, **Argimiro Aguilar** (Plaza del Ayuntamiento 7; www.argimiroaguilar.com). **El Mercado de la Pulga** (San Fernando 22) has a more alternative and eclectic selection of novelties.

The Language of the Fan

Hand-operated air-conditioner, fashion statement, art canvas and even advertising hoarding, the Spanish fan served and continues to serve many functions but none more successfully than that of text messager. In the days when young men and women were forbidden to talk to each other directly without going through a chaperone, a language of fans evolved so that from a distance ladies were able to communicate their desires and arrange trysts from balconies or behind grilles or across ballrooms without anyone else knowing what was being said. There was even an alphabetical fan code which enabled words to be spelled out letter by letter, though due to its complexity it was rarely used. Those in the mating game, however, would be in no doubt as to the meaning of a fan wafted across the heart (I love you), a half-open fan held over the face (they're watching us!) or the holding up of the fan to shield the face from the sun (you're ugly!).

Fine Food and Wine

Any large supermarket will stock a range of Valencian and Spanish products. However, the best place to go for fresh produce and spices – and for a spot of people-watching – is without doubt the **Mercado Central** *(see page 39)*.

A specialist fan maker

For wines not available in supermarkets, there are several high-class specialist wine shops. These also double as delicatessens, selling fine cheeses, hams, olive oils, *turrón* (a traditional Spanish nougat eaten at Christmas) and other gourmet Spanish products. **Bodegas Segui** (Pianista Amparo Iturbi 16), near the Mercado de Russafa, and **Mantequerías Castillo** (Gran Via Marqués de Turia 1) are both family-owned and of long pedigree. **Mantequerías Piquer** (Cirilo Amorós 33) has also been open for a long time, although not under the same ownership; it is known for its cheeses as much as its wines. Other good shops for wines are **Monastrell** (Jaime Beltrán 21), **Las Añadas de España** (Játiva 3) and **Bouquet** (Burriana 44), the latter specialising in the wines of Valencia province.

Most *pastelerías* have a good choice of sweet things to try. There are sweet shops in Calle Muro de Santa Ana, beside the Torres de Serranos. **Trufas Martinez** at Calle Ruzafa 12 sells delicious chocolate truffles.

Paella Pans

If you are inspired to go home and cook your own paella, you'll need the proper pan to do it, and possibly a cooking

Paella pan shop near the Mercado Central

support for it or gas ring – it is important that heat reaches all of the pan evenly. Paella pans come in a range of sizes, from tiny to enormous, and they are classed according to how many people they will serve. The easiest place to find them is outside the **Mercado Central**. You can buy the ingredients inside the market at the same time.

Furniture and Antiques

Valencia holds an international furniture trade fair every year and has a wide range of shops in Sedavi, Alfafar, Benetuser and Beniparrell. For classic and avant-garde furniture, try **Añil** at Gran Via Marqués del Turia 22; www.anilmuebles.com.

Calle Músico Peydrò (parallel with San Vicente Mártir) is known for its wicker, cane, bamboo and pine furniture and ornaments. Shops include **Cestería el Globo** at No. 16.

Antiques shops and dealers are concentrated in the old town in streets such as Avellanas, Baja and Purisima.

ENTERTAINMENT

During the city's frequent fiestas you won't be short of entertainment. There's plenty to do the rest of the year, whether your taste is for a formal concert or a casual night of bar-hopping. To find out what's on in Valencia see the weekly listings magazine *Cartelera Turia*, available from newsstands.

Music

The principal venues for performances of classical music, opera and ballet are the **Palau de la Música** (Paseo de la Alameda 30, tel: 96 337 50 20; www.palaudevalencia.com) and the four halls in the **Palau de les Arts** (tel: 902 202 383; www.lesarts.com; *see pages* 56), which is located in the City of Arts and Sciences.

Rock, pop, jazz and blues are more often to be found in more intimate venues such as the **Black Note Club** (Polo and Peyrolón 15, tel: 96 393 36 63; www.blacknoteclub.com).

Theatre and Cinema

Most theatrical performances are in Spanish or Valencian, although occasionally international companies do perform. The main theatre is **Teatro Principal** (Barcas 15, tel: 96 353 92 00 for tickets; www.teatres.gva.es).

Almost all films, whether shown at the cinema or on television, are dubbed into Spanish, but **Filmoteca Generalitat Valenciana** (IVAC, Plaza del Ayuntamiento 17, tel: 96 353 93 00) and **Albatros** (Plaza Fray Luis Colomer 4, tel: 96 393 26 77) often show foreign films in their original language with subtitles (look for 'VO' – *version original* – on posters). Most cinemas have three or four showings a day from 4pm to 11pm. Every October Valencia hosts an international festival of film, showcasing films from the countries around the Mediterranean; www.mostravalencia.com.

Nightlife

Valencia is well known for its nightlife – the so-called Luna de Valencia (Moon of Valencia) – nurtured by its benign outdoor climate. Most of the action is in bars called *pubs* which are not at all like their British namesakes: in Spain, *pubs* have minimalist décor, loud (sometimes live) music and few seats. They don't open until late – the young rarely begin a night out before 11pm – and stay open till the early hours. Most *pubs* won't close before 3am and discos before 5am.

Broadly, Valencia's nightlife can be divided into four zones. The **Barrio del Carmen** *(see page 36)* is said to be favoured by bohemians, and offers some historical atmosphere to enjoy between drinks. Two well-known bars worth having a drink in are **Negrito** (on Plaza del Negrito) and **Bolsería** (Calle Bolsería 41).

The bars around the Plaza Cánovas del Castillo, on the Gran Via Marqués del Turia, on the other hand, are upmarket and the haunt of the city's rich kids. The two other pleasure zones along Calle Juan Lorens (near the Mercado de Abastos) and in an area to one side of the football stadium (the avenidas of Aragón and Blasco Ibañez, and the Plaza de Xúquer) are in the modern parts of town. For an altogether more elegant – and expensive – night out there is the **Gran Casino Monte Picayo**, a ten-minute drive from Valencia.

La madrugada

The prime nightlife time, the small hours of the morning from midnight to daylight, is called *la madrugada*. It comes from the Spanish word, *madrugar*, meaning to get up very early.

Gays and lesbians have their own night-time haunts. Starting points for men could be the restaurants with floor shows **Pekado** (Plaza Vicente Iborra 9 in the Barrio del Carmen) and **Turangalila** (Calle del Mar 34), and for women **Mogambo** (Sangre 9), beside the city hall.

FIESTAS

Spanish fiestas have to be seen to believed, and Valencia does them particularly well. Most are inspired by a religious pretext, although sometimes this is not readily apparent. If you do find yourself here during a fiesta, forget about doing everything else except enjoying it: streets are likely to be cut off, some shops and museums closed and restaurants and public transport full – but there will not be a dull moment.

All dressed up for Las Fallas

Las Fallas

The big fiesta of the year in Valencia is Las Fallas, from 12 to 19 March. It's very noisy but also very spectacular, and if you want to know Valencia you have to see it at least once. Hotels are usually fully booked months in advance. The fiesta supposedly originated in medieval times when the city's carpenters would burn their rubbish in the streets outside their workshops on the arrival of spring.

The first week of March, in the lead-up to Las Fallas, there are great processions of people in traditional costume and a *mascletà* – a daylight firework display – in the Plaza del Ayuntamiento every day at 2pm. Then from 12 March until the end it is noise and commotion all the way. There are concerts in the streets, paella-making competitions, bullfights and people letting off fireworks whenever they feel like it.

On the night of 15–16 March hundreds of *fallas* are put in place throughout the city. Each *falla* – which may be up to 25m (80ft) high – is a set-piece sculpture making a satirical point; figures called *ninots* form mini-scenes within the *falla*. Teams of artists take a whole year to design and build the wood, papier-mâché and fibre-glass figures. To see as many *fallas* as possible, go to a newsstand for a copy of *El Turista Fallero*, which includes a map. The best *fallas* are classed as *sección especial*.

The days of 17 and 18 March are dedicated to the patroness of Valencia, the Virgen de los Desamparados, and a giant floral sculpture of her is made in the Plaza del Virgen. On the night of the 18th there is a firework display in the riverbed. The climax of Las Fallas occurs at midnight on the 19th, when the *fallas* are filled with fireworks and set alight one by one. Last to go up in flames is the biggest *falla* of all, the one in the Plaza del Ayuntamiento, in front of the city hall.

Easter Week (Semana Santa)

The fishing quarter of El Cabanyal stages colourful processions from Palm Sunday to Easter Sunday. Around 5,000

The Fallas Makers

If Las Fallas seems like a waste of otherwise good pieces of art (and money), consider this: which other city is able to generate an endless supply of work for its artists? A permanent colony of them is kept busy in the 60 workshops of the Ciutat Fallera in Benicalap, knowing whatever wonderful creations they dream up and take a year to painstakingly build will be reduced to ashes the following 19 March. Fortunately, a handful of *ninots*, the comic figures that populate the *fallas*, are saved from the flames by a vote each year and placed on display in the Museo Fallero (see page 55).

people, organised into 27 *cofradias* or brotherhoods, take part. Many of them dress as Biblical characters while others appear as Roman soldiers or, anachronistically, in the uniforms of Napoleonic grenadiers.

The best processions to see are the Silent Procession at midnight on Maundy Thursday and the slow, solemn Procession of the Burial of Christ on Good Friday, which starts around 6pm. The Procession of the Resurrection on Easter Sun-

Flowers are a major part of Valencian fiestas

day is a more joyful affair, during which the participants throw flowers to the spectators.

Corpus Christi

The Corpus Christi parade (on a date between mid-May and mid-June, depending on the date of Easter) sets off in the late afternoon to the sound of the *tabalet* (drum) and *dolçaina* (a kind of flute) and does a circuit of the streets in the old part of the city around the cathedral. It is essentially an ecclesiastical parade centring upon the great monstrance that is normally kept in the cathedral museum, but the whole occasion is surrounded by colourful traditions. Over 270 people take part as costumed Biblical personalities, giants, *cabezudos* (carnival figures with overlarge heads), eagle-people and *cirialots* who carry tall candles. In the midst of all of them is la Moma, a person dressed in white with the face covered by a Venetian mask, who symbolises virtue victoriously resisting the seven deadly sins who dance around him or her. An essential part of the procession are the 10 *rocas*, mobile stages on which mystery plays were once performed.

July Fair *(Feria de Julio)*

This summer celebration has nothing to do with religion and everything to do with livening up the city during a month when citizens are tempted to abandon it for the country or the beach – at least that was the rationale for the 19th-century city council to create it. Most events take place in the Paseo de la Alameda and in the Viveros garden. They include fireworks; rock, pop and jazz concerts; theatre; ballet; and a brass-band competition. There is also a calendar of first-class bullfights in the bullring. The climax, on the last Sunday of the month, is a battle of flowers in the Alameda: an hour of gentle carnation throwing.

SPORTS

Spectator Sports

The great spectator sport in Valencia is **football**. The city's internationally successful team, Valencia CF, plays at the Campo del Mestalla, in Avenida de Suecia (tel: 96 360 17 10), a stadium with a seating capacity of 55,000. Valencia's other team is Levante UD.

Bullfighting takes place at the Plaça de Bous (Plaza de Toros; tel: 96 351 93 15), near the main railway station. If you want to see a fight it is best to go with someone who can explain what is going on and to be prepared for what you see: the ritualised killing of animals in an unequal fight. Tickets can be surprisingly expensive and get booked up quickly for important *corridas*. Cheaper seats are in the sun *(sol)*; the more expensive in the shade *(sombra)*.

The European Grand Prix is raced on the Formula 1 circuit laid out around the port. Cheste, due west of Valencia on the Madrid road, has a **motorcycle** racing circuit. **Cycling** competitions take place at the Velódromo Luis Puig; **basketball** is played in the Pabellón Fuente de San Luis.

Participant Sports

The **parklands** of the Turia riverbed *(see page 46)* are available year-round for anyone who wants to jog, cycle, rollerblade, skateboard, practise athletics or play football. Another good place for jogging or cycling is the Paseo Maritimo beside the beach *(see page 63)*.

For **swimming** there are Valencia's beaches in summer and the indoor swimming pool, Piscina Valencia (Paseo de la Alameda 21, tel: 96 360 47 08), in winter. For **horse riding**, contact La Hípica at Calle Jaca 23 (tel: 96 361 53 63). **Tennis** players can practise at the University Campus of Universitat de Valencia (Menéndez and Pelayo 19, tel: 96 354 32 36). The Real Club Náutico de Valencia (Camino del Canal 91, tel: 96 367 90 11) co-ordinates **yachting** activities.

Campo de Golf de El Saler

There are six **golf** courses within Valencia province. The closest to the city is Campo de Golf de El Saler (Los Pinares, El Saler, tel: 96

161 11 86), which has been ranked as one of the 50 best golf courses in the world. Other courses near the city are those of El Bosque, Manises and Escorpión.

VALENCIA FOR CHILDREN

Children are universally welcomed in Spain at any time of day or night. There are, however, seldom special allowances or facilities for them such as high chairs and children's portions in restaurants, but waiters and other staff will generally go out of their way to help.

If hiking around the monuments of the city is not for your children, a compromise may be to take a ride on the Bus Turistic or in a horse-drawn carriage, both departing from the Plaza de la Reina. Some sights may please both adults and kids. The obvious ones are the **City of Arts and Sciences**, especially **L'Hemisfèric** IMAX cinema and **L'Oceanogràfic** with its shows of performing dolphins, and the **Bioparc** at the **Parque de Cabecera**. A surprisingly child-friendly museum is the **Museo de Historia de Valencia** *(see page 48)*, which has life-size display screens. The bed of the River Turia

Dolphins at L'Oceanogràfic

has lots of space to play, and a giant climbing frame-cum-slide in the shape of Gulliver is near the Puente del Angel Custodio.

A kids' treat for a long day out from Valencia is a visit to **Terra Mitica** theme park near Benidorm (tel: 90 202 02 02, www.terra miticapark.com), around an hour and a half each way by motorway.

Calendar of Events

5 January Cabalgata de Los Reyes – parade in honour of the Three Kings who arrive on this day bringing children their Christmas presents.

17 January St Antony's Day – pets and other animals are taken to be blessed by a priest on a podium in Calle Sagunto.

22 January Procession in honour of St Vincent the Deacon, co-patron of the city.

12–19 March Las Fallas – festival culminates on 19 March with the ceremonial burning of giant figures *(see page 89)*.

Semana Santa (Easter Week) Processions in the Cabanyal *(see page 90)*.

San Vicente Ferrer (Sunday and Monday after Easter) Children act out the miracles of St Vincent Ferrer on a stage set up near his birthplace at the end of Calle de la Mar.

May Fiesta de La Virgen de los Desamparados (second Sunday in May) – festival in honour of Valencia's patroness; a statue of the Virgin is carried in procession from her basilica to the cathedral.

May or June Corpus Christi procession takes place in the streets of the old city around the cathedral *(see page 91)*.

23–24 June Fiesta de San Juan (St John's Night) – with bonfires on the beach.

July (all month) Feria de Julio – July Fair, ending with the battle of the flowers on the last Sunday *(see page 92)*.

August (last Wednesday) La Tomatina – a battle with tomatoes in the town of Buñol, west of Valencia; (last Sunday) La Cordá – a spectacular firework festival in Paterna outside Valencia.

September (first week) Grape harvest festival in the wine-growing region of Requeña.

9 October Fiesta de la Comunitat Valenciana – commemoration of the reconquest of Valencia in 1238 by Christian forces with a procession carrying the regional flag leaving from the city hall.

Mid-October Mediterranean Film Festival.

1 November Día de Todos Los Santos (All Saints' Day/Day of the Dead) – people decorate the city's cemeteries with flowers.

EATING OUT

Eating out is one of the great pleasures of a visit to Valencia. Not only does the city have a huge range of fresh produce but also the climate to make it possible to have a meal outdoors for much of the year.

The city's numerous restaurants range in atmosphere from laid-back to formal. Dishes native to other parts of Spain can be sampled, but most restaurants describe themselves as offering Valencian cuisine which, as much as referring to a number of emblematic, rice-based dishes, effectively means making optimum use of the freshest of ingredients available at the local market, fish and seafood being foremost among them.

Mealtimes

Mediterranean Spain's eating hours vary greatly from those of the rest of Europe. For many visitors, the late mealtimes can take some getting used to. Breakfast *(desayuno)* is of little importance. Many Spaniards will have only a light meal first thing in the morning – a few biscuits or a piece of toast with a milky coffee, or perhaps a glass of fresh orange juice in a bar. They save their appetites for a proper breakfast mid-morning, around 10.30 or 11am. It is at this time you will see bars and cafés packed with people tucking into a sandwich or piece of toast for *almuerzo*.

The city's shops and offices close at around 1 or 1.30pm (which to the Spanish is midday) and the bars fill up again, this time for tapas and a beer or wine. First-time visitors are often alarmed at how long Spaniards put off lunch *(la comida)*, the main meal of the day – most restaurants won't even open until 1.30pm and will not start filling up until well after 2pm. It is considered acceptable to sit down for a meal at

Feasting at La Fonda in Plaza de la Reina

3.30pm, a time when the rest of Europe is halfway through the afternoon. The Spanish, of course, consider that everyone else in Europe eats too early, and they claim that their late lunchtime allows them to get a full morning's work done.

Anyone who has the opportunity will prolong lunch over coffee, and perhaps brandy and a cigar, and then put their feet up for the *sobremesa*, the lazy digestion time after lunch or even have a siesta, especially if it is a hot day in summer.

At 4 or 5pm the afternoon *(la tarde)* begins. Many people fill the long haul between lunch and dinner with a visit to a café or a *pastelería*, at 6 or 7pm, for something sweet. This stop-gap meal is called *la merienda*.

Some foreign visitors feel they are wasting away by the time restaurants open for dinner/supper *(la cena)*. Only those places geared up for tourists will be open before 8pm. Around 9pm is a more usual time to dine, and many locals may not even sit down to dinner until after 10pm. However, there are plenty of bars in Valencia where you can eat tapas, and fast-food restaurants open for long hours without a break in the middle of the day.

Paella

Valencia's speciality is paella, Spain's most famous dish. It is eaten wherever the occasion presents itself, but although there are take-away versions for eating in the streets it is usually kept as a semi-special treat for an office outing or as a way to bring the family together on a weekend. It is at its best when it forms part of a leisurely lunch (never dinner) with friends: it is a meal to share and the dish itself can be a good icebreaker for conversations.

An ingenious combination of ingredients which can look as good as it tastes, paella originated as a simple dish that the labourers of the *huerta* could prepare over an open fire during the rice harvest using one shallow, round pan. The first paellas were flavoured with eels – abundant in the wetlands around the Albufera – and eaten communally, straight from the dish, each person with a wooden spoon working his way through an allotted segment, courteously respecting his neighbours' portions.

Paella Etiquette

Don't trust any restaurant that offers you an instant paella; proper paella is a dish that needs to be served as soon as it is cooked. You will normally be asked to order at least half an hour in advance, stating how many people it is for (usually a minimum of two). As you finish your appetisers the paella will be brought to your table for your approval and served in front of you. It is best eaten with a squirt of lemon and no accompaniments, except a salad and a pitcher of beer or bottle of wine. Don't be afraid to use your fingers to attack the chunks of meat.

Over time, the checklist of ingredients for a good paella resolved itself into the recipe for the *paella valenciana*. As well as rice, a truly authentic paella is made with chicken, rabbit and snails – although you can consider the last item as optional.

Purists will allow a *paella marinera*, made from seafood instead of meat, but they regard with abhorrence the so-called *paella mixta*, combining the two in the same dish.

The two principal vegetables in paella are *bajoqueta* (green beans) and *garrofó* (a large, pale butter bean). Two

Dishing up paella

other beans – *ferraura* and *tavella* – are sometimes used as well, and artichokes are added by some chefs. Rosemary lends its distinctive perfume to the simmering rice, as does saffron, which also turns the rice yellow. Nowadays, almost everyone below gourmet level substitutes cheap artificial colouring for the expensive saffron and the dish comes out tasting just as good.

No other ingredients are needed. Peas, tomatoes, peppers, garlic, sausages and the million and one other 'improvements' that slip into bogus paellas across Spain and in foreign countries have no place in the genuine article. They seldom enhance the appearance of the dish and they certainly create a confusion of tastes.

Churros, a favourite with hot chocolate in winter

Paella is cooked in a particular kind of metal pan (widely available in Valencia in a variety of sizes), by preference over a wood fire but in practice usually over a gas ring. The important thing is for the pan to be level and the heat evenly distributed from centre to rim. Although there are recipes to follow, it takes the skill and intuition of an experienced cook to add the right amount of stock and let it simmer over an even heat, just long enough for the paella to reach the table with the rice cooked to the point of tenderness, neither dry and crunchy, nor moist and mushy. Really good paellas even have a light layer of delicious semi-burnt crust beneath the rice, called *socarrat*, which has to be scraped off the bottom of the pan: paella afficionados consider this a delicacy.

Other Local Specialities

Paella is not the only thing on a Valencian menu, it should be emphasised; Valencia excels at rice dishes in general. One of the most popular after paella is *arroz a banda*, rice cooked in fish stock. This was originally a way of using tasty but bone-ridden fish which were inadvertently trapped in nets and not worth the fuss of eating individually. In restaurants nowadays, good-quality fish is used for the dish, and this will be served separate to the rice, accompanied by *all i oli*, a garlic-flavoured mayonnaise.

Arroz al horno (*arros al forn* in Valencian) has an altogether different taste, being an oven-baked dish made with chick peas, pork, potato, sausage, tomato, garlic and black pudding. In the days before domestic ovens, housewives would prepare this dish in an earthenware casserole and take it to the local baker's to have it cooked. Yet another variation on the theme of rice is *arros negre* (black rice), which is made with squid, the ink giving the dish its colour and name.

If you want a change from rice, in the La Safor region around Gandía they make *fideuà*, a kind of seafood paella in which the rice is replaced with vermicelli. In the Albufera, look on the menu for *all i pebre d'anguiles* – a stew made with eels, garlic and paprika. Another typical Valencian dish, perhaps more modest, is the cold salad, *esgarrat*, made with red peppers, dried salt cod and olive oil.

As for sweets, Valencians are expert in turning almonds into all things delicious. *Turrón* (nougat) and *mazapanes* (marzipan), favourite Christmas treats, are made in Alicante, inland from the Costa Blanca. The town of Casinos, in the hills northwest of Valencia, is known for its *peladillas* – whole almonds covered in sugar. Other delights to be found in *pastelerías* (cake shops) are *rollitos de anis* (aniseed-flavoured biscuits),

Churros

A favourite Spanish snack, eaten mostly in winter, is *chocolate con churros*: thick hot drinking chocolate into which is dunked sugared, deep-fried batter sticks (*churros*).

rosegones (small, hard almond biscuits), *pasteles de bonia-to* (pies of sweet yam) and *susus*, sticky doughnuts filled with a creamy custard. At Easter, soft and subtly sweet *panque-mado*, literally 'burnt bread' but in reality something akin to brioche, makes a good breakfast or goes well with an afternoon coffee.

Tapas

Tapas are little, appetizing snacks ordered at the bar to accompany a glass of wine or beer – Spaniards will rarely be seen drinking without eating something to go with it. Because tapas are available all day, they are a good way to fill gaps between meals or, if you order enough of them, to replace a meal altogether. But be careful: although it seems like an inexpensive way to eat, you can easily run up a larger bill than expected and pay more for an evening of tapas than you would have done for a *menú del día* (set menu). It's cheaper, by the way, to eat at the bar than to have a seat at a table.

There is rarely a tapas menu that can be brought to the table to study. Some items may be chalked up on a board or else the barman or waiter will reel off a long list of them and, if you are lucky, explain what they are. The simplest thing is to point to anything you fancy displayed on the counter. If you are stumped, all bars everywhere will serve you a wedge of *tortilla de patata* (potato omelette), a scoop of marinaded olives or a few slices of cheese *(queso)* or *jamón serrano* (cured ham).

The daily menu

Wine and tapas at the counter

If you want something more substantial than a tapa, ask for the same dish as a *ración*, which is always at least double the size of a tapa and often much more. You can also ask for an in-between quantity, a *media ración*. Almost anything that can be served as a tapa can just as easily be put into a baguette to make a *bocadillo* (sandwich) to eat in or take away.

Wine and Other Drinks

Valencian vineyards are generally not well known outside the region, but they are gradually making a reputation for themselves. Those of Utiel and Requeña, the main growing areas, produce some good rosés and medium-strength dry reds. The cold continental climate of Valencia's Alto Turia district, meanwhile, favours dry white wines.

If you bar-hop your way around Valencia, you'll almost certainly come across something a little stronger: Agua de

A city bar and restaurant

Valencia, a cocktail of sparkling wine, orange juice and vodka which slips down all too easily.

If you prefer something non-alcoholic, Alboraya just outside Valencia (see page 68), is the birthplace of a refreshing summer drink popular all over Spain, *horchata*, a sweet milky drink made from crushed tubers (called tigernuts). In the city centre, the best places to try it are two *horchaterías* opposite each other off Plaza de la Reina, Santa Catalina and El Siglo (see page 29), but the best place to drink it is in Alboraya, specifically in the *horchatería* Daniel. *Horchata* is always served cold and you can ask for it as a liquid *(liquida)* or semi-frozen *(granizada)*. You can drink it straight or copy the locals and dunk soft sweet cake sticks *(fartons)* or crunchy breadsticks *(rosquilletas)* into it. Although you can now buy packaged *horchata* all year round in supermarkets, it is not comparable to the fresh product. Another drink served by cafés and *horchaterías* is *leche merengada*, a kind of milkshake with egg and sugar added and flavoured with lemon and cinnamon.

Horchata-making often goes with ice cream and Valencia has a reputation in Spain for producing the country's best ice creams, a skill supposedly derived from its historical connections with Italy.

TO HELP YOU ORDER

Could we have a table?	**¡Nos puede dar una mesa, por favor?**
Do you have a set menu?	**¡Tiene un menú del día?**
I'd like a/an/some…	**Quisiera…**
The bill please	**La cuenta, por favor (El compte, per favor)**

MENU READER

agua	water	**entremeses**	hors-d'oeuvre
al ajillo	in garlic	**gambas**	prawns
a la plancha	grilled	**helado**	ice cream
al punto	medium	**jamón serrano**	cured ham
arroz	rice		
asado	roasted	**judías**	beans
atún	tuna	**langosta**	lobster
azúcar	sugar	**leche**	milk
bacalao	salt cod	**mariscos**	shellfish
bocadillo	sandwich	**mejillones**	mussels
boquerones	anchovies	**pan**	bread
bien hecho	well done	**patatas**	potatoes
buey/res	beef	**pescado**	fish
calamares	squid	**picante**	spicy
cangrejo	crab	**poco hecho**	rare
caracoles	snails	**pollo**	chicken
cerdo	pork	**postre**	dessert
cerveza	beer	**pulpitos**	baby octopus
champiñones	mushrooms	**queso**	cheese
chorizo	spicy sausage	**ternera**	veal
cocido	stew	**tortilla**	omelette
cordero	lamb	**verduras**	vegetables
ensalada	salad	**vino**	wine

PLACES TO EAT

We have used the following symbols to give an idea of the price for a three-course meal for one, including wine, cover and service:

€€€€ over 60 euros   €€ 20–30 euros
€€€ 30–60 euros   € below 20 euros

CITY CENTRE

RESTAURANTS

Albacar €€€ *Sorni 35, tel: 96 395 10 05, www.restaurante albacar.com.* Located in a street off Calle Colón heading for the riverbed, this is a highly rated restaurant serving Mediterranean-based cuisine. Typical dishes include lasagne with prawns and vegetables. If you are in doubt as to what to order you can order a selection of small taster dishes *(raciones)* which will typically include oysters with pork and ham, and artichokes with cod and clams, and for dessert mango and ginger-filled horns and a profiterole with cream cheese and honey ice cream. Closed Saturday lunchtime, Sunday, Easter week and August.

Ana Eva € *Turia 49, tel: 96 391 53 69, www.restauranteanaeva.es.* Ana Eva serves good, inexpensive vegan cuisine in informal surroundings near the Torres de Quart. For starters try the *ensalada silvestre* made with beansprouts and mixed varieties of lettuce, for main course mushrooms with tofu in a basil sauce, and for dessert crème caramel made with carob flour. Closed Sunday night and Monday.

Joaquín Schmidt €€€ *Visitación 7, tel: 96 340 17 10, www. joaquinschmidt.com.* Chef Joaquín Schmidt Río-Valle has created a very personal restaurant, somewhere between cutting edge and classic but still charming and intimate. There's a very good wine list, and the service is impeccable. Choose between three set menus of varying sizes and prices. The largest, and most expensive, the 'Joaquín Schmidt Menu', allows you to sample seven dishes, as well as cheese and dessert. Closed Monday lunch, Sunday and last two weeks of August.

La Carme €–€€ *Sogueros 8, tel: 96 392 25 32.* Open evenings only. A no-nonsense, inexpensive place to eat in the northern part of the Barrio del Carmen. The three-course menu allows little choice, but all the food is freshly prepared and with a touch of imagination.

La Riuà €€ *Calle de la Mar 27, tel: 96 391 45 71.* La Riuà has been serving home cooking by a husband and wife team since 1982. Their Valencian cuisine includes a wide range of rice, fish and shellfish dishes, and the restaurant is particularly acclaimed for its paella, other rice dishes, *fideua* and *all i pebre*. Best to book in advance at this legendary restaurant.

La Sucursal €€€ *IVAM, Guillem de Castro 118, tel: 96 374 66 65, www.restaurantelasucursal.com.* As the cafeteria-restaurant of the modern art museum, this is a place that revels in an unashamedly contemporary cuisine. Closed Sunday, Saturday lunchtime, Easter and first half of August.

Seu Xerea €€€ *Calle Conde de Almodovar 4, tel: 96 392 40 00, www.seuxerea.com.* A meeting of Mediterranean, British and Oriental cuisines in a slick restaurant not far from the Plaza de la Virgen. Starters might include mussels in green curry or Thai-style fishcakes, while mains might be tuna in teriyaki sauce or slow-roast lamb with cumin sauce; finish with a coconut sorbet. At lunchtimes there is a cheap *menú del día*. Much more pricey is the excellent *menú de degustación* (taster menu). Closed Saturday lunchtime and Sunday.

Taberna Alkazar €€€ *Mosén Femades 11 (Zona Peatonal), tel: 96 352 95 75.* The Alkazar is an up-market seafood and paella restaurant that first opened its doors in 1950. Choose a table inside or outdoors in the pedestrianised street. There's a busy tapas bar if you don't feel like a full meal. Large selection of wines. Closed Monday, Easter week and August.

TAPAS BARS

Note: it is difficult to give a guide price for bars as the bill will vary enormously according to what you order.

100 Montaditos € *Plaza de la Reina 10, tel: 96 391 92 27*. One of a chain of bars in a traditional style which specialise in inexpensive tapas, especially, as the name says, 100 different kinds of open sandwiches or *montaditos*.

A Fuego Lento €–€€ *Caballeros 47, tel: 96 392 18 27*. A high-class and high-priced tapas bar with a contemporary feel. Good choice of hams and cheeses. Closed Sat lunch and Sunday.

El Pilar € *Moro Zeit 13, tel: 96 391 04 97*. One of the oldest tapas bars in the city, dating from 1912, and as famous as ever for its mussels.

ALONG THE RIVER

A Tu Gusto €–€€ *Escritor Rafael Ferreras (on the corner with Avenida Instituto Obrero), tel: 96 322 70 26, www. atugusto.com*. Relaxed place a few streets away from the City of Arts and Sciences where you can enjoy creative Mediterranean dishes and a very good value lunch-time menu. Closed Sunday, Monday and Tuesday.

El Angel Azul €€–€€€ *Conde Altea 33, tel: 96 374 56 56, www. restaurantedangelazul.com*. The 'Blue Angel', near the Puente de Aragón, serves highly rated Mediterranean cuisine in elegant surroundings. There is a reasonably priced *menú del día* and a more expensive taster menu. Closed Sunday, Monday and August.

Marisquerías Civera €€€ *Mosén Femandes 10, tel: 96 347 59 17, www.marisqueriascivera.com*. Fish and seafood restaurant of long standing in the historic centre of the city. Apart from the seafood, there are also some meat and vegetarian options. Closed Sunday night and Easter week.

Submarino €€€ *L'Oceanogràfic, City of Arts and Sciences, tel:
96 197 55 65.* Relatives of the fish on your plate swim around
you at this novelty underwater restaurant at the L'Oceanogràfic
aquarium, which also serves rice dishes. Reservation is essential.
Closed Sunday evening.

THE SEAFRONT

RESTAURANTS

Ca'Sento €€€€ *Calle Méndez Nuñez 17, tel: 96 330 1775.* This
is widely regarded as Valencia's best restaurant, largely because
of its use of prime ingredients treated with subtlety and creat-
ivity. It's worth saving space for the desserts. A meal here can
easily add up to a substantial sum, and if you want to keep the
price in check, it's safest to go for the *menú degustación* (taster
menu). Book in advance. Closed Sunday, Monday night, Easter
and August.

L'Estimat €€–€€€ *Paseo de Neptuno, 16, tel: 96 3 71 10 18
www.restaurantlestimat.com.* You can eat gazing out to sea in
this restaurant, which is one of the more traditional ones on the
Playa de las Arenas beach. It has been serving paellas and other
rice dishes since 1927.

La Pepica €€–€€€ *Paseo Neptuno 2, 6 and 8, www.lapepica.
com, tel: 96 371 03 66.* A classic Valencian restaurant founded in 1898 and visited by Ernest Hemingway and other writers, as well as bullfighters, artists and assorted VIPs. It is
situated on a street along the beach which is lined with paella restaurants – some cheaper and where, arguably, you can
eat just as well. La Pepica is known not only for its rice dishes but also for its lobster stew and grilled fish. Closed Sunday.

La Rosa €€–€€€ *Paseo Neptuno 70, tel: 96 371 20 76.* Not as
well known as La Pepica, this is another good place to eat paella
while watching the waves at sea. Also good for fish and seafood.
Large menu and a good wine list. Closed August.

Taj Mahal €–€€ *Doctor Candela 20, tel: 96 330 62 64.* This Indian/Pakistani restaurant is in the suburbs between the city and the seafront (between Avenida del Puerto and Avenida Blasco Ibáñez). All the spices are imported from the Indian subcontinent. It is decorated with handicrafts and paintings, not least, of course, on the theme of the Taj Mahal.

TAPAS BAR

Casa Montaña €€ *José Benlliure 69, tel: 96 367 23 14, www. emilianobodega.com.* This tapas bar, which was founded in 1836, has been turned into a tasting centre for fine wines. Around a thousand types from around the world, but especially Valencia, can be ordered by the glass. All the dishes on the menu are made from carefully selected ingredients and include mussels, grilled sardines, squid, anchovies, typical Cabañal recipes, codfish croquettes, and different Spanish cheeses and cold meats. Closed Sunday evening.

OUTSKIRTS

Alquería Del Pi €€–€€€ *Camino Viejo de Godella 55, tel: 96 365 17 70, www.alqueriadelpi.com.* A traditional Valencian farmhouse of the *huerta* standing in a 19th-century Mediterranean garden. Off a small road heading north out of the city.

El Rek €€ *Pintor Martí Girbés 1, El Palmar, tel: 96 162 02 97, www.elrek.com.* El Rek is located outside the town of El Palmar, in the heart of Valencia's rice-growing area and beside La Albufera. The menu consists of traditional Valencian cuisine, including paella, *arroz a banda* and *arroz negro*. The restaurant has its own landing stage for boat trips around the lake.

La Matandeta €€€ *Carretera Alfafar–El Saler km 4, Alfafar (7km/4 1/2 miles from Valencia), tel: 96 211 21 84.* Fresh fish and seafood are served in a typical country house in the *huerta*. Here you get a chance to taste paella cooked over an open wood fire, which gives the dish a delicious smoky flavour.

Raco' Nou €€€ *Carretera de El Palmar 21, El Palmar tel: 96 162 01 72.* Typical Valencian cuisine at this long-established restaurant – including rice dishes, seafood and *all i pebre* – served beside La Albufera.

BUNOL

La Venta de l'Home €€€ *Ventamina, tel: 96 250 35 15, www. lahoya.net/ventalhome (50km/31 miles west of Valencia: take the Ventamina exit from the Valencia–Madrid motorway after passing Buñol).* At around 300 years old, this former staging post on the old road to Madrid is the oldest restaurant in the Comunidad Valenciana. There is a *menú gastronómico* to sample a bit of everything (the menu varies according to seasonal availability) and, if you have the time for a leisurely meal, a more expensive *menú especial*. Note that the price of the two menus doesn't include drinks.

CULLERA

Casa Salvador €€€ *L'Estany de Cullera, tel: 96 172 01 36, www.casasalvador.com.* Casa Salvador is in two *barracas* (typical Valencian farmhouses) next to a freshwater lake used for fish farming. It is a family business which claims to have been open every day for the last 50 years. Choose from a wide range of rice and fish and other typical Valencian dishes, including *arroz negro* and whole fish baked in a salt crust. There's an outdoor terrace overlooking the lake.

DENIA

El Poblet €€€–€€€€ *Urbanización El Poblet 43, Carretera Les Marines, tel: 96 578 41 79, www.elpoblet.com.* El Poblet is considered one of the very best restaurants in the Valencian region for its creative adaptation of Medirreanean cuisine. There's a sampler menu *(menú de degustación)* available for patrons wanting to taste a range of dishes. Closed Sunday night and Monday, 25 February–15 March, and 20 November–1 December.

GANDIA

La Casona €€€ *Irlanda (Urbanización San Nicolás between Gandía and its beach), tel: 96 284 59 59, www.restaurantela casona.es.* A wide selection of starters introduces a main-course menu of fish, meat and rice dishes all with fresh vegetables of the season. Homemade desserts. There's a garden with outdoor tables. Closed Mon, Tue–Thur evenings and Sun evening.

PENISCOLA

Casa Jaime €€€ *Avenida Papa Luna 5, tel: 96 448 00 30, www. casajaime.net.* The menu is mainly strong on rice dishes and fresh fish from the coast of Castellón. Closed Sunday night, Wednesday in winter and 20 December–20 January.

SAGUNT

L'Armeler €€–€€€ *Subida al Castillo 44, tel: 96 266 43 82, www.larmeler.com.* Sagunt's best restaurant is in the old Jewish quarter, on the way up out of the old town towards the Roman theatre and the castle. It serves a combination of Valencian and French cuisine with dishes on the menu including wild boar with chestnut purée and mushroom gratin flambéed.

XATIVA

Casa La Abuela €€€€€€ *Calle Reina 17, tel: 96 228 10 85, www.casalaabuela.es.* "Grandmother's House" has changed over its 50-year existence from a simple restaurant into an establishment renowned for its cooking, still based on traditional local recipes, particularly Valencian rice dishes.

A–Z TRAVEL TIPS

A Summary of Practical Information

A

ACCOMMODATION (*hoteles, alojamiento*; see also CAMPING, YOUTH HOSTELS and RECOMMENDED HOTELS on page 139)

Spanish hotels are awarded one to five stars according to their facilities – a system that tells you nothing about quality, views or the history of the building, let alone intrinsic personality. Hostels (*hostales*, denoted by the letter H outside) and *pensiones* (boarding houses, denoted by the letter P) are more modest types of hotel with fewer facilities. Both are graded with one to three stars. The letter R suffixed to a hotel or hostel sign means *residencia* and indicates that there is no restaurant.

Valencia's best hotels get booked up quickly for trade fairs and the Fallas festival in March. In general, prices are quoted per room (as opposed to per person) and breakfast is not included. Value added tax (IVA) may or may not be included so it is best to confirm this. When checking in you will be asked to surrender your passport for a short period while the details are copied from it.

I'd like a double/single room.	**Quisiera una habitación doble/individual**
with/without bath/shower	**con/sin baño/ducha**
double bed	**cama de matrimonio**
What's the rate per night?	**¿Cuál es el precio por noche?**
Is breakfast included?	**¿Está incluido el desayuno?**

AIRPORTS (*aeropuerto*; see also GETTING THERE)

Valencia's international airport is at Manises (tel: 96 159 85 00), 8.5km (5 miles) from the city centre. You can get to the centre by Aero-Bus. Services depart every 20 minutes 6am–10pm and cost €2.50. There are stops on Avenida del Cid (by the police station) and Calle Ángel Guimerá (junction with Calle Juan Llorens). Alternatively, you can take metro lines 3 or 5 to the centre; line 5 goes all the way to the port via a tram link *(see also page 136)*. Taxis line up outside the arrivals hall and charge around €20 for the ride into the centre.

B

BEACHES *(playas)*

Valencia's warm climate means that the many long, sandy beaches accessible from the city can be enjoyed for several months of the year. They get busy during the Spanish holiday period of July and August (especially the latter), and at weekends in June and early September.

The **Playa de Las Arenas** and **Playa de la Malvarrosa** together comprise the city's main beach, which is easy to reach from the city centre by buses 1, 2, 19, 20, 21 and 22 or the tramway (metro line 4). A wide swathe of fine golden sand, it is good for bathing.

The two most popular beaches to the north of Valencia are **La Pobla de Farnals** and **Port Saplaya**, both within easy reach by car. To the south the principal beaches are **Playa de Pinedo** (6km/ 4 miles from Valencia) and **Playa del Saler** (12km/7½ miles), which are reached by taking the motorway to the town of El Saler and then the coast road, CV-500. There is also a bus service there.

BICYCLE HIRE

Valencia is an ideal city for cycling around, being flat and with a warm, dry climate, and there's an excellent network of cycle lanes. The local transport company (www.metrovalencia.com) provides information on 14 'Bicimetro' cycle routes that can be accessed using the metro. Bicycles can be hired from the following:

Ecotours Cyclos at Gran Vía Marqués del Turia 15, tel: 67 662 20 63, www.cyclotourbike.com; also hires two- and four-seater, pedal-powered cars.

Orange Bikes Manuel Aguilar 1, tel: 96 391 75 51, www.orange bikes.net.

Do You Bike Plaza Horno de San Nicolás, tel: 96 315 55 51, www.doyoubike.com.

Valencia Guías Paseo de la Pechina 32; tel: 96 385 17 40, www.valenciaguias.com. Guided bicycle tours around the city.

BUDGETING FOR YOUR TRIP

Transport to Valencia. For Europeans, Valencia is a short and direct scheduled flight away from many major cities. Budget operators have made flying within Europe much more competitive; however, if you are travelling from beyond Europe the flight will be a considerably greater proportion of your overall budget.

Accommodation. Hotels in Valencia are quite expensive, but many offer special off-peak deals. A cheaper, though less convenient, option is to stay outside Valencia. See price guides in the 'Recommended Hotels' section, starting on *page 139*. It is always wise to book ahead.

Meals. Restaurant prices are not cheap, though with favourable exchange rates, even top-rated restaurants may be surprisingly affordable compared to many European capitals. The *menú del día*, a fixed-price midday meal, is an excellent bargain available in most restaurants, even fancy ones. Spanish wines are reasonably priced.

Local Transport. The sights in the city centre are mostly within walking distance of each other, making public transport use often unnecessary. Public transport in Valencia is inexpensive and even taxis are an affordable way to get around.

Museums. Many of Valencia's museums and galleries charge for admission. Note that many institutions are free on Sundays and closed on Mondays. See also Valencia Tourist Card *(below)*.

Valencia Tourist Card. This card permits the holder to travel free on public transport and gives discounts on entry to museums and other tourists sights, entertainment venues, shops and restaurants. It is available in one-, two- or three-day forms for €12, €18 and €22 respectively, from tourist information offices, bus stations, hotels and tobacconists. For more details, tel: 90 070 18 18; www.valenciatouristcard.com.

C

CAMPING

Valencia's climate makes camping quite easy for most of the year. There are three campsites to the south of the city, not far from the sea and close to the Albufera nature reserve: **Camping Coll-Vert**, Playa de Pinedo, Carretera Nazaret-Oliva km 7.5, tel: 96 183 00 36; **Camping Devesa Gardens**, Carretera del Saler, km 13, tel: 96 161 11 36, www.devesagardens.com; and **Camping Puzol**, Playa de Puzol, tel: 96 142 15 27, www.campingpuzol.com.

CAR HIRE (*coches de alquiler*, see also DRIVING)

You won't need a car to move around the city because the transport system is so good and, besides, finding a parking space is often tricky. But if you decide to make trips beyond the urban area you'll find your own transport will give you more flexibility.

The Spanish company **Atesa** (www.atesa.es) has an office at Valencia airport (tel: 96 152 35 88), as do the major international car-hire companies, including **Avis** (tel: 96 152 21 62, www.avis.es); **Hertz** (tel: 96 152 37 91, www.hertz.es); and **Europcar** (tel: 96 152 18 72, www.europcar.es).

To hire a car you must be over 21 and have had your driving licence for at least six months – citizens of the EU can use their normal licences; other nationals need an international one.

I'd like to hire a car	**Quisiera alquilar un coche**
tomorrow	**para mañana**
for one day/a week	**por un día/una semana**
Please include	**Haga el favor de incluir**
full insurance.	**el seguro a todo riesgo.**
unleaded petrol	**gasolina sin plomo**
Fill it up.	**Lleno, por favor.**

CLIMATE

Valencia receives sunshine for most of the year, and has an average annual temperature of 17°C (63°F). The best seasons to visit are spring and autumn, although sometimes there is light rainfall in both. Summers can be hot and humid, but winters are mild, with a temperature which rarely falls below 10°C (50°F). The average monthly highs and lows are given below:

	J	F	M	A	M	J	J	A	S	O	N	D
°C	13	14	16	18	21	25	28	28	25	21	16	13
	6	7	9	11	14	18	21	21	19	15	11	8
°F	55	57	60	65	71	78	82	82	77	69	62	56
	43	45	48	52	57	65	69	69	66	58	51	46

CLOTHING (ropa)

Valencians like to dress up. Although men are expected to wear jackets in elegant restaurants, smart-casual clothes will do most of the time. In the summer not many people go to restaurants wearing shorts unless the restaurant happens to be right on the beach. Women visiting churches should show respect by not wearing shorts or clothing that's too revealing. You will need a warm jacket from November to March, or a sweater and raincoat.

CRIME AND SAFETY (see also LOST PROPERTY)

Valencia is not a particularly dangerous place, but caution should be practised at all times as in any big city, especially in crowded metros or bars. Areas around the harbour or the Malvarrosa neighbourhood can be dangerous at night and it is advisable to avoid small, unlit streets and parks everywhere after dark.

Otherwise precautions are: never leave your bags unattended; don't carry too much money with you; wear your camera strapped to your body; and photocopy your personal documents and leave the originals in your hotel's safe, along with your valuables. Don't leave anything on display inside your car.

If you are the victim of a robbery, go to the nearest police station *(comisaría)* and make a report *(denuncia)*; you will need it for your insurance claim. For the local police, call 092.

I want to report a theft.	**Quiero denunciar un robo.**
My ticket/wallet/passport has been stolen.	**Me han robado mi billete/ cartera/pasaporte.**

D

DRIVING

When driving in Spain you must carry with you the following documents: your passport, a valid driving licence, registration papers and a Green Card (international insurance certificate) with a bail bond from your insurance company.

Road conditions. Outside of the morning and evening rush hours, Valencia's roads aren't too congested for a big city. However, there are big traffic jams on entry roads into the city on Sunday evenings and after holiday weekends.

Motorways. Valencia city and province are well served by main roads and motorways. The A7 motorway coming from the north (Catalonia) and going towards the south (Alicante) is a toll road *(autopista)*. The motorway that goes to the west (Madrid) is toll-free *(autovía)*.

Rules and regulations. You should display a nationality sticker on your car. Most fines for traffic offences are payable on the spot. Driving is on the right and overtaking (passing) is on the left. Give right of way to vehicles coming from the right (unless your road is marked as having priority). The use of front and rear seat belts is compulsory.

Speed limits in Spain for cars are 120km/h (75mph) on motorways, 100km/h (62mph) on broad main roads (two lanes each way), 90km/h

driving licence	**carnet de conducir**
car registration papers	**permiso de circulación**
Can I park here?	**¿Se puede aparcar aquí?**
Are we on the	**¿Es ésta la carretera**
right road for…?	**hacia…?**
Where does this road lead?	**¿Adónde va esta carretera?**
Fill the tank please,	**Llénelo, por favor,**
top grade.	**con super.**
petrol	**gasolina**
unleaded petrol	**gasolina sin plomo**
diesel	**gasóleo**
Please check the oil/	**Por favor, controle el aceite/**
tyres/battery.	**los neumáticos/la batería.**
I've broken down.	**Mi coche se ha estropeado.**
There's been an accident.	**Ha habido un accidente.**

(56mph) on other main roads, 50km/h (31mph), or as marked, in densely populated areas.

Always carry your driving licence and/or international driving permit with you. As the police can demand to see your passport at any time, it is also a good idea to carry a photocopy of its important pages.

Spanish law requires that your car should carry a set of spare headlamp and rear-lamp bulbs and that you wear a reflective yellow safety jacket (to be kept in the front of the car) before you step out of the car in the event of a roadside emergency. Seat belts are compulsory and children under the age of 10 must travel in the rear.

Breakdowns. Spanish garages are efficient and spare parts are readily available for most common makes of car. If you are an affiliated member of the RAC, you may call on the services of the Real Automóvil Club de España, tel: 90 240 45 45 (roadside assistance), which has its Valencia headquarters at Gran Vía Marqués de Turia 79, tel: 96 334 55 22.

Road signs. Some of the street names and signs are in Valencian. Most essential road signs, however, use the standard European pictographs. The translations below could be useful:

¡alto!	stop!
aparcamiento	parking
autopista (de peaje/peatge)	(toll) motorway (expressway)
ceda el paso	give way (yield)
curva peligrosa	dangerous bend
despacio	slow
desviación	diversion (detour)
estacionamiento prohibido	no parking
obras	roadworks
¡pare!	stop!
peatones	pedestrians
peligro	danger
salida	exit (from motorway)

E

ELECTRICITY *(corriente eléctrica)*

The standard is 220-volt, though if you are in an old building you may find 125-volt current. If in doubt, check before plugging in any of your appliances. Sockets take round, two-pin plugs, so you will probably need an international adapter plug. Visitors from North America will need a transformer unless they have dual-voltage travel appliances.

EMBASSIES AND CONSULATES *(embajadas y consulados)*

All embassies are in the national capital, Madrid.
Australia: Paseo de la Castellana 259D, tel:91 353 6600; www.spain.embassy.gov.au

Canada: Paseo de la Castellana 259D, tel: 91 382 8400; www.canadainternational.gc.ca
Ireland: Paseo de la Castellana 46–4, tel: 91 436 4093
New Zealand: Pinar 7, tel:91 523 0226; www.nzembassy.com/spain
South Africa: Calle de Claudio Coello 91–6, tel: 91 436 3780
UK: Paseo de la Castellana 259D, tel: 91 714 6300; www.ukinspain.fco.gov.uk
US: Serrano 75, tel: 91 587 2200; www.embusa.es
Some countries have consulates in Valencia, including:
UK: Colón 22 (5th floor), tel: 96 352 07 10
US: Doctor Romagosa 1 (2nd floor), tel: 96 351 69 73

EMERGENCIES

National Police *(policía nacional)*, in and outside Valencia: **091**
Local police *(policía local)*: **092**
Fire *(bomberos)*: **080**
Emergencies *(emergencias)*: **112**
Guardia civíl (outside the city): **062**

Fire!	¡Fuego!
Help!	¡Socorro!
Stop!	¡Deténgase!
Call the police/	Llame a la policía/
an ambulance	una ambulancia
Where is the nearest	¿Dónde está el hospital
hospital?	más próximo?

G

GETTING THERE

By air. Valencia's airport *(see page 115)* receives direct scheduled flights from airports across Spain and Europe. Flights from the rest of the world go via Madrid and Barcelona. Spain's national carrier is Iberia (tel: 96 902 400 500, www.iberia.es). The low-cost carriers with flights to and from Valencia are Ryanair (www.ryanair.com) and easyJet (www.easyjet.com)

By sea. Valencia port (www.valenciaport.com) has a ferry line to the Balearic Islands operated by Trasmediterránea Estación Marítima (tel: 90 245 46 45, www.trasmediterranea.es).

By rail. Valencia is linked by rail with the main Spanish cities and with European cities via Barcelona. There are daily trains to Madrid, Seville, Alicante, Barcelona, Port Bou (the French border), Zaragoza and Bilbao. Spain's train company, RENFE (tel: 90 232 03 20 in Spain, tel: 90 224 34 02 international, www.renfe.es), operates two stations in Valencia: **Estación del Norte** (the main one) and **Estación del Cabañal**, near the seafront.

By car. The region's principal routes, the A7 motorway (the Autopista del Mediterráneo, toll-paying except for the Valencia by-pass) and the N340 (north) and N332 (south) run along the coast. The latter two tend to be congested with lorries and they pass through many small towns, making the motorway by far the best option if you can afford it.

A toll-free motorway, the A3, connects Valencia with Madrid. Other major roads are the A23 to Teruel and Zaragoza and the A35 (south) motorway to Xàtiva, becoming the A31 to Albacete.

By coach (long-distance bus). Valencia's coach/bus station, the Estación de Autobuses (Avenida Menéndez Pidal, tel: 96 346 62 66), is next door to the Nuevo Centro shopping centre on the north bank of the Turia riverbed. It has coach links with the main Valencian and Spanish cities, and some European cities via Barcelona. From the coach station, you can take a local bus or the metro to get to the city centre.

GUIDES AND TOURS

Guided tours. There are guided tours of the historical centre of Valencia in English every Saturday from 10am to noon starting in the Tourist-Info in the Plaza de la Reina, tel: 96 385 17 40, www. valenciaguias.com. Prices: €15 (adult), €7.50 (child).

Bus turistic. This tourist bus takes two interesting routes, one around the city centre; the other out to La Albufera. You can get on and off it at any stop, and recorded commentary is in English and other languages. Buses leave the Plaza de la Reina every hour from 10.30am to 7pm (March–Dec). The bus costs €14 per adult and €8 per child from 6 to 12; children under 6 travel free. You can buy tickets in advance at www.valencia-on-line.com.

We'd like an English-speaking guide.	**Queremos un guía que hable inglés.**
I need an English interpreter.	**Necesito un intérprete de inglés.**

H

HEALTH AND MEDICAL CARE

Residents of the European Union should carry with them the European Health Insurance Card or EHIC, available from post offices or online at www.ehic.org.uk, which entitles them to free medical treatment within the EU. It is unwise to travel without health insurance as treatment can be expensive.

Be careful not to overdo the sunbathing in the first couple of days. Falling asleep on the beach is a common cause. Take the sun in short doses for at least the first few days, using a high-factor sunscreen; and drink plenty of bottled water (*agua mineral*) to avoid dehydration.

If you need a doctor in an emergency, call 112, or go to the **Hospital Universitario La Fe** (Avenida de Campanar 21) or the **Hospital Clínico Universitario** (Blasco Ibañez 17).

For non-emergencies, you may be able to solve the problem by visiting a *farmacia*, a chemist's shop, indicated by a green cross sign. Pharmacists are trained to give advice on treating common ailments and sometimes can prescribe without consulting a doctor. *Farmacias* are open during normal shopping hours. Out of hours, there is always one designated *farmacia de guardia* open in a neighbourhood: its address will be posted in the window of other *farmacias*. *Parafarmacias* are something else: these are shops which sell baby food, beauty products, and a few non-prescription drugs, but the staff are not pharmacists qualified to give advice.

Where's the nearest (all-night) chemist?	¿Dónde está la farmacia (de guardia) más cercana?
I need a doctor/dentist.	Necesito un médico/dentista.
It hurts here.	Me duele aquí.
an ambulance/hospital	una ambulancia/un hospital
sunburn	quemadura del sol
sunstroke	insolación
a fever	fiebre
an upset stomach	dolor de estómago
insect bite	una picadura de insecto

L

LANGUAGE

Valencia has two official languages, Valencian *(valenciano)*, which is a variant of Catalan, and Spanish, more properly called Castilian *(castellano*, that is, the language of Castile). Both are legally recognised by the Spanish constitution and are used daily. Many street names are in Valencian, and official papers are usually in both languages. Overleaf are some common phrases in both Valencian and Castilian.

English	Valencian	Castilian
good morning/good day	bon dia	buenos días
good afternoon/good evening	bona tarda	buenas tardes
goodnight	bona nit	buenas noches
please	si us plau	por favor
thank you	gràcies	gracias
you're welcome	de res	de nada
goodbye	adéu	adiós

LOST PROPERTY

If you lose an item of value, report the loss to the Municipal Police or the Guardia Civíl (see POLICE). Ask for a copy of the police report, which you will need to make an insurance claim once you are home.

I've lost my wallet/ handbag/passport.	He perdido mi cartera/ bolso/pasaporte.

M

MAPS (planos)

The tourist information office gives out good maps of the city centre, but if you want to visit the outskirts you will probably have to buy a more detailed map in a bookshop. **Regolf** (Calle de la Mar 22, tel: 96 392 23 62) is a specialist map shop. If you are thinking of walking in the countryside, you may want to buy a 1:50,000 army map.

One manifestation of the upheavals that post-Franco Valencia has been undergoing is in the changing names of streets and squares, some of which have been confusingly re-baptised. The Plaza del

Ayuntamiento, for example, was previously called the Plaza del Caudillo, after the rank Franco gave himself. Sometimes locals will refer to the old name of a street or square when giving directions. Here are a few *valenciano* street signs:

English	Valenciano	Castilian
avenue	avinguda	avenida
street	carrer	calle
church	església	iglesia
palace	palau	palacio
boulevard	passeig	paseo
square	plaça	plaza
a street plan of...	un plano de la ciudad de...	
a road map of...	mapa de carreteras de...	

MEDIA

Major British and continental newspapers are on sale the same day as publication in newspaper kiosks in the city centre, as well as in the train station and the airport.

There are seven main Spanish TV channels, most dedicated largely to sport, foreign films and game shows. Better-equipped hotels receive non-Spanish satellite TV channels. Travellers with short-wave radios will be able to pick up the BBC World Service and the Voice of America.

Have you any English-language newspapers?	¿Tienen periódicos en inglés?

MONEY *(dinero)*

Currency. The monetary unit of Spain is the euro (**€**); with one hundred cents making 1 euro. Coins: cents 1, 2, 5, 10, 20 and 50, and euros 1 and 2. Banknotes: euros 5, 10, 20, 50, 100, 200 and 500.

Banking hours are usually Monday–Friday 9am–2pm. Automatic Teller Machines *(cajeros automáticos)* are everywhere, and from them you can draw funds in euros against your bank account with a credit/debit card, although your bank may charge a handling fee.

Changing money. Many travel agencies display a *cambio* sign, meaning they will change foreign currency. Most hotels will also change money, albeit at a slightly less favourable rate than at the bank. Traveller's cheques always get a better rate than cash. Take your passport with you when changing money.

Credit cards and **traveller's cheques** are accepted in most hotels, restaurants and big shops.

Where's the nearest bank?	**¿Dónde está el banco más cercano?**
I want to change some pounds/dollars	**Quiero cambiar libras/dólares**
Do you accept traveller's cheques?	**¿Acepta usted cheques de viaje?**
Can I pay with this credit card?	**¿Puedo pagar con esta tarjeta de crédito?**

OPENING TIMES

Shops. Usual opening hours are Monday–Saturday 10am–1.30pm and 5–8.30pm. The big department stores open all day 10am–9pm. Shops are closed on Sundays except on special occasions such as the run-up to Christmas.

Post offices. Generally open Monday–Friday 9am–2pm and Saturday 9am–1pm.

Banks. Usually open Monday–Friday 9am–2pm.

Government offices and most businesses. Open Monday–Friday 9am–2pm and 4–8pm. In summer, many offices operate from 8am–3pm only to avoid the hottest part of the day.

Restaurants. Mealtimes in Spain are later than in the rest of Europe. Breakfast is served between 7.30 and 10am. Lunch is 2–3.50pm, and dinner generally 9–11pm.

Museums. Generally, these are open Tuesday–Saturday 9am–1pm and 4–8pm and Sunday morning, and are closed Monday.

Entertainment venues. Most cinemas have several showings a day between 4pm and 11pm. Some theatres offer two performances a day at 6pm and 10pm. Pubs and musical venues are open between 9pm and 3am and discos 11.30pm–5am.

P

PHOTOGRAPHY *(fotografía)*

All popular types of discs, cards and batteries are widely available. Wherever possible, ask people for their permission before you take their picture. It is forbidden to take photographs of any military bases, military or naval port areas, police or military personnel.

POLICE *(policía)*

Valencia has two kinds of police force: the national police *(policía nacional)*, dealing with serious crime, and the local police *(policía local)* in charge of public order. Spain has a third police force, the civil guard (Guardia Civíl), which operates in the countryside and patrols the main roads. In Valencia, dial **092** for the local police and **091** for the national police. The police station at the city centre is

Where's the nearest   ¿Dónde está la comisaría
police station?   más cercana?

located near the river, opposite Los Viveros gardens, at Calle Los Maestres 2, tel: 96 353 97 25.

POST OFFICES (correos)

Spanish post offices have white and yellow signs saying 'Correos y Telégrafos'. You can send mail but not phone from them. They are usually open Monday–Friday 9am–2pm and Saturday 9am–1pm. If you just need stamps, get them from any tobacconist (estanco). Mail boxes (buzón de correos) are yellow.

Valencia's main post office is at Plaza del Ayuntamiento 24, tel: 96 351 23 70. It is open Monday–Friday 8.30am–8.30pm and Saturday 9.30am–2pm.

Where is the (nearest) post office?	¿Dónde está la oficina de correos (más cercana)?
Have you received any mail for…?	¿Ha recibido correo para…?
A stamp for this letter/ postcard, please	Por favor, un sello para esta carta/tarjeta
express (special delivery)	urgente
airmail	via aérea
registered	certificado

PUBLIC HOLIDAYS (fiestas)

1 January	**Año Nuevo**
6 January	**Epifanía (Día de Reyes)**
22 January	**San Vicente Mártir**
19 March	**San José** **(Las Fallas)**
1 May	**Fiesta del Trabajo**
15 August	**Asunción de Nuestra Señora** **(Virgen de agosto)**

9 October	**Día de la Comunidad Valenciana**
12 October	**Día de la Hispanidad**
1 November	**Todos los Santos**
6 December	**Día de la Constitución**
8 December	**La Inmaculada Concepción**
25 December	**Navidad**

Movable dates:

Viernes Santo	Late March/April
Lunes de Pascua	Late March/April
San Vicente Ferrer	Late March/April

R

RELIGION *(religión; servicios religiosos)*

The national religion of Spain is of course Roman Catholicism, and mass takes place in almost all the city's churches. Anglican services are held on Sunday mornings at the Iglesia de Jesucristo, Calle Dos de Abril 36, tel: 96 344 43 07, www.iglesiaepiscopal valencia.4t.com.

For details of Muslim worship contact Centro Cultural Islámico de Valencia, Arquitecto Rodriguez 17, tel: 96 360 33 30, www.webcciv.org.

The Jewish community is served by the Javurá synagogue (Calle Uruguay 59, door 13, tel: 96 380 21 29, www.uscj.org/world/valencia), which is affiliated to the United Synagogue of Conservative Judaism and the World Council of Conservative Synagogues.

T

TELEPHONES *(teléfono)*

Spain's country code is **34**. Valencia's provincial area code, **96**, must be dialled before all phone numbers, even for local calls.

You can make local, national and international calls from public phone booths *(cabinas)* in the streets, which operate with coins or cards. Instructions are given in several languages and some admit international credit cards. Phone cards *(tarjetas telefónicas)* can be purchased at tobacconists *(estancos)*,post offices or newsstands.

You can also make calls at public telephone centres called *locutorios* which are quieter than phone boxes and more convenient than fiddling with coins, as you pay over the counter when you have finished your call. Calls from a hotel room are usually more expensive than calls from phone boxes or *locutorios*. If you must phone from your hotel, ask in advance how much a three-minute call will cost. Reversed charge calls (collect) made to European Union countries can be dialled directly, otherwise they must be made through the operator.

To make an international call, dial **00** + country code + phone number, omitting the initial zero. The country code for the UK is **44,** for US and Canada **1**, for Australia **61** and for Ireland **353**.

Calls are cheaper after 10pm on weekdays, after 2pm on Saturday and all day on Sunday.

For national and international information dial **11888**. You can also find phone numbers at www.paginasamarillas.es and www.paginasblancas.es. For any other information on telephoning in Spain, see www.telefonica.es.

TIME ZONES

Spanish time coincides with that of most of Western Europe: Greenwich Mean Time plus one hour. In spring, clocks are put forward an hour, maintaining the one-hour difference.

New York	London	**Spain**	Sydney	Auckland
6am	11am	**noon**	8pm	10pm

TIPPING *(propinas)*

A service charge is normally included in hotel and restaurant bills, and tipping is not obligatory, but it is the normal practice to leave a little small change on a bar counter or restaurant table. If you want to tip a taxi driver, 5 percent will be enough, unless he or she has been especially helpful. A common Spanish way of tipping in all circumstances is to round up the bill to the nearest euro or so.

TOILETS *(servicios)*

There are not many public toilets in Valencia. Usually the most convenient option is to use those in a department store like El Corte Inglés, or in a bar or café – in the latter cases, it is polite to buy a drink.

In Spanish there are several words for toilets, the most common are *servicios, aseos* and *lavabos*.

TOURIST INFORMATION *(oficina de turismo)*

The main tourist offices for the city are:

Calle de la Paz 48, tel: 96 398 64 22. Open Monday–Friday 9am– 8pm, Saturday 10am–8pm and Sunday and public holidays 10am–2pm. For information about the city and the whole Valencian region.

Plaza de la Reina 19 (next to Santa Catalina church and the tourist bus stop), tel: 96 315 39 31. Open Monday–Saturday 9am–7pm and Sunday and public holidays 10am–2pm.

Estación del Norte (the main railway station), tel: 96 352 85 73.

Tourist Info-Diputación, Poeta Querol (near the Teatro Principal), tel: 96 351 49 07 for information about Valencia province.

Airport (arrivals hall), tel: 96 153 02 29.

Tourist-Info Beach, Paseo de Neptuno 2 (in front of Hotel Neptuno), Mon–Fri 10am–7pm, Sat–Sun 10am–6pm (open in summer only).

TRANSPORT *(transporte público)*

Valencia has a fast and reliable public transport network reaching almost everywhere a visitor would want to go. Fares are quite reasonable, too.

By bus. Valencia's fleet of red buses is operated by EMT (Empresa Municipal de Transportes de Valencia), tel: 96 315 85 15, www.emtvalencia.es. There are 91 routes during the day and seven night ones. At most bus stops there are maps of the city with all the routes marked. A single-trip bus ticket costs €1.25, but if you are going to be using buses a lot, buy a *bonobus* (€6), valid for 10 trips, from a tobacconist's *(estanco)*.

By metro and tramway. Valencia's metro network is run by FGV (Ferrocarriles Generalitat Valenciana). Modern, clean and reliable, it is organised into six lines (Nos 1, 3, 4 and 5) that link the city centre with nearby towns:

Línea 1: Lliria (northwest) and Bétera (north) to Torrent (southwest) and Villanueva de Castellón (near Xàtiva, 40km/25 miles) to the southwest).

Línea 3: Rafelbunyol (north) to the Airport (west).

Línea 4: Ll. Larga-Terramelar (north) and Mas del Rosari (north) to Doctor Lluch (east). This line is a modern tramway serving the city's beaches – depart from Pont de Fusta station.

Línea 5: Marítim Serrería (east) to the Airport (west) and Torrent (southwest). A tram connects Marítim Serrería with the port (Neptú).

When is the next bus/train for…?	**¿A qué hora sale el próximo autobús/tren para…?**
I want a ticket to…	**Quiero un billete para…**
What's the fare to…?	**¿Cuánto es la tarifa a …?**
single (one-way)	**ida**
return (round-trip)	**ida y vuelta**
Where can I get a taxi?	**¿Dónde puedo coger un taxi?**

The main interchanges are Empalme, Benimaclet and Angel Guimera. The network is mainly designed to meet the needs of residents and commuters; apart from the new airport connections (lines 3 and 5), only one line (No. 4), going in one direction, is of much use to tourists. The network will continue to expand in the coming years with the building of lines 2 and 6.

Fares are from €1.40 for a single ticket and from €6.50 for a *bonometro*, a ticket valid for 10 trips. For more information, tel: 90 046 10 46 or see www.metrovalencia.com.

By taxi. Taxis (always white cars) are everywhere and are not too expensive. You can hail one in the street or go to a taxi rank. It may be hard to find one during the peak periods of 8–9pm and 1–2pm. A green light or a *libre* sign shows that a taxi is available for hire. There are two kinds of tariff: one for daytime (6am–10pm) trips within the urban area; the other for night time and journeys outside the city limits.

Taxi companies include the following: Onda-Taxi, tel: 96 347 52 52; Radio-Taxi, tel: 96 370 33 33; Valencia Taxi, tel: 96 374 02 02; Taxis Toledo, tel: 96 352 72 05; and Tele-Taxi, tel: 96 357 13 13.

V

VISAS AND ENTRY REQUIREMENTS

Most visitors, including citizens of all EU countries, the US, Canada, Australia and New Zealand, require only a valid passport – not a visa or a health certificate – to enter Spain.

Visitors from South Africa should apply in advance for a Schengen visa, and passports should be valid for at least three months beyond the expiry date of your visa. If you expect to remain for longer than 90 days (180 days if you're a US citizen), a Spanish consulate or tourist office can advise you of the necessary steps to take.

WEBSITES AND INTERNET ACCESS

Many hotels in Valencia have internet connections and there are many areas of the city covered by Wifi.

www.turisvalencia.es The most comprehensive website on Valencia, in various languages.

www.valencia.es The city hall's site.

www.valencia-on-line.com Another useful general site (also a booking agency).

www.valenciaterraimar.org Information on Valencia province.

www.comunitatvalenciana.com Information on the region, including the Costa Blanca and Costa del Azahar.

www.spain.info Spain's national tourism website.

is advisable to take a taxi back to your hotel.

YOUTH HOSTELS

Valencia has two youth hostels for the use of hostelling card holders (Hostelling International):

Albergue Juvenil Center Valencia, Calle Samaniego 18, tel: 96 391 49 15, www.alberguejuvenilvalencia.com. Offers 2, 4, 6 and 8 bed accommodation.

Albergue La Paz, Puerto 69, tel: 96 361 74 59, www.alberguela paz.org.

For more information, contact Red Española de Albergues Juveniles, Calle Castelló 24, Int-6°-decha, 28001 Madrid; tel: 91 522 7007, www.reaj.com.

Recommended Hotels

Spanish hotels are graded one to five stars depending upon facilities. Some establishments are classified as *hostales* (with one to three stars) and others *pensiones* – these are not necessarily less welcoming or less comfortable than a hotel of higher rank. The suffix *residencia* to a hotel or *hostal* means that there is no dining room, although breakfasts may still be served.

In a class of their own are *paradores*, state-run hotels which either occupy historic buildings or are purpose-built in privileged locations. Either way, a *parador* offers a reliable level of comfort and its restaurant specialises in the cuisine of the region. El Saler is the *parador* closest to Valencia; the next closest are Jávea on the Costa Blanca and Benicarló on the Costa del Azahar.

The following guide indicates prices for a double room in high season. These should be used as an approximation only as prices can vary widely and even expensive hotels can sometimes offer competitive deals for weekend stays.

€€€€	over 200 euros
€€€	120–200 euros
€€	80–120 euros
€	below 80 euros

CITY CENTRE

Ad Hoc Monumental €€€ *Calle Boix 4, tel: 96 391 91 40, www.adhochoteles.com.* A charming little three-star hotel in a sensitively restored late 19th-century mansion on the edge of the old town near the river (between the Torres de Serranos and the Gobierno Civil). It has great character with its patio garden, exposed brickwork and beams, high ceilings and eclectic mixture of antique and modern furniture. Very close to the riverbed and the Museo de Bellas Artes (Museum of Fine Arts). 28 rooms.

Antigua Morellana € *Calle En Bou 2, tel: 96 391 57 73, www. hostalam.com.* A small family-run hotel in an 18th-century building in a little street between La Lonja and Plaza de la Reina. The staff are friendly and some of the rooms have been newly refurbished. No dining room but there are restaurants not far away. Good value. 18 rooms.

Astoria Palace €€€–€€€€ *Plaza de Rodrigo Botet 5, tel: 96 398 10 00, www.hotel-astoria-palace.com.* Located on a small square in the city centre, close to the Plaza del Ayuntamiento, the Astoria Palace is a big, luxurious and somewhat impersonal hotel of long standing. It has a range of rooms and suites as well as business and fitness centres, a restaurant and a bar. 204 rooms.

Chill Art Hotel Jardín Botánico €€–€€€ *Dr Peset Cervera 6, tel: 96 315 40 12, www.hoteljardinbotanico.com.* This small hotel is, as its name suggests, close to the botanic gardens, a little way from the city centre proper. There is a gym and sauna as well as a café. 16 rooms.

Consul del Mar €€€ *Avenida del Puerto 39, tel: 96 362 54 32, www.hotelconsuldelmar.com.* Conveniently located a short way up the street towards the port from the Palau de la Música is this four-star hotel in a building from the early 20th century. It has a heated indoor pool, sauna and gym. Some of the rooms are in the attic. 57 rooms.

Home Deluxe Hostel € *Calle Louja 4, tel: 96 391 62 29, www.likeathome.net.* A cheap and sociable guesthouse aimed at budget travellers – one step up from a youth hostel – and conveniently located in one of the old streets south of Calle Caballeros. The same organisation has a cheaper youth hostel for backpackers on Calle Vicente Iborra. Both establishments have a guest kitchen, internet access and multilingual staff, and are open 24 hours a day. 10 rooms.

Hospes Palau de la Mar €€€ *Calle Navarro Reverter 14, tel: 96 316 28 84, www.hospes.es.* Completely renovated and featuring a contemporary, minimalist décor, this boutique hotel is sited within two 19th-century mansions on a busy street between the old town and the river. As well as a high-season rate, it has an extra-high season rate for important trade fairs and sporting fixtures. The restaurant serves a variety of the finest Valencian cuisine. 66 rooms.

Inglés €€–€€€ *Marqués de Dos Aguas 6, tel: 96 351 64 26, www.hotelinglesvalencia.com.* A modern, three-star chain hotel behind the 19th-century façade of the former mansion of the Cardona family. Centrally located next to the Palacio del Marqués de Dos Aguas (Ceramics Museum). Some rooms have large balconies. 63 rooms.

Melia Valencia €€€ *Calle Menorca 22, tel. 96 335 03 80, www.melia-valencia.com.* A sumptuous five-star hotel with spacious rooms looking over the gardens in the bed of the River Turia. A little far from the city centre, it is well located for a visit to the City of Arts and Sciences. There is a terrace and pool on the roof. 196 rooms and 10 suites.

Reina Victoria €€–€€€ *Barcas 4–6, tel: 96 352 04 87, www.husareinavictoria.es.* A few minutes' walk from the railway station, and overlooking Plaza del País Valenciano, this is Valencia's grandest hotel. The art-nouveau establishment, which opened in 1913, still has an old-fashioned feel, although it has been modernised. Over the years, the roll-call of distinguished guests has included Picasso, Dalí, García Lorca and Miró, as well as King Alfonso XIII and Queen Victoria. La Pérgola restaurant serves a buffet lunch. For a quiet drink there is the English-style Victoria bar. 97 rooms.

Venecia €–€€ *En Llop 5, tel: 96 352 42 67, www.hotelvenecia.com.* At the top (narrow) end of Plaza del Ayuntamiento with some rooms overlooking the square. The train station is just a three-minute walk away. The recently refurbished rooms are relatively plain with minimal decor, but clean and comfortable with a small bathroom. Internet access is available and there is an individual safe in each room. Rooms have been adapted for disabled guests. 54 rooms.

SEAFRONT

Las Arenas €€€ *Eugenia Vines 22–24, tel: 96 312 06 00, www.hotel-lasarenas.com.* A five-star spa resort on the Paseo Marítimo incorporating elements of a 1930s spa, including the swimming pool. It has large lounges and a garage, restaurants and a café-bar. 253 rooms.

Neptuno €€€ *Paseo Neptuno 2, tel: 96 356 77 77, www.hotel neptunovalencia.com.* A modern luxury hotel on the beach next to a line of restaurants specialising in paella. Rooms have hydromassage baths, plasma TV screens and internet access. About 10 rooms face the sea; book early to get one. Restaurant, gym, jacuzzi and sauna. 47 rooms.

OUTSKIRTS

Ad Hoc Parque Golf €€–€€€ *Urbinazación Torre en Conill 6–8, Bétera (20km/121/2 miles from Valencia), tel: 96 169 83 93, www.adhochoteles.com.* A rural hotel belonging to the owners of the city centre Ad Hoc Monumental. Located opposite the Escorpión Golf Club Garden. Garden terrace and swimming pool. 40 rooms.

La Calderona Spa and Golf Resort €€€€ *Calle Botxi 2–4 Urbanización Torre En Conill Bétera (20km/12½ miles from Valencia), tel: 96 169 94 00, www.lacalderona.com.* Five-star hotel for sports lovers and fitness fanatics where if you have to ask the price you can't afford it. Arrange for a personal fitness routine or play golf in the adjacent Escorpion golf course. 42 rooms.

Mas de Canicatti €€€ *Carretera Pedralba km 2.9, Vilamarxant (25km/151/2 miles from Valencia), tel: 96 165 05 34, www.masdecanicatti.com.* A small hotel complex in an estate of citrus groves which grows eight varieties of mandarin and two of orange which are harvested from October to March. The main building is an old country house or *masía*. An extension to this contains the spa, business centre and El Càdec restaurant which serves classic

Valencian cuisine. The suites, some of them with private swimming pool, are located in independent outbuildings. 27 rooms.

Hotel La Mozaira €€€ *Camí del Machistre 50, Alboraya, tel: 961 85 09 24, www.lamozaima.com.* A renovated 17th-century whitewashed *alquería*, not far from the city and only a 10-minute walk from the sea. It stands in the *huerta* and is surrounded by tigernut fields, the ingredient of Valencia's famous summer drink, *horchata*. The restaurant serves organic vegetables from the hotel's own garden.

Parador de El Saler €€€ *Avenida de los Pinares 151 (18km/11 miles from the city centre by motorway; 17km/10 1/2 miles from the airport), tel: 96 161 11 86, www.parador.es.* Part of the state-run chain of plush hotels, this is an elegant refuge from the city next to a nature reserve and the sea, and surrounded by an internationally known golf course. The restaurant serves paella and other typical Valencian dishes. 58 rooms. Bookings can be made directly with the *parador* or via Paradores de Turismo de España, Requena 3, 28013 Madrid, tel: 90 254 79 79 or the *paradores'* agent in the UK, Keytel International, The Foundry, 156 Blackfriars Rd, London SE1 8EN, tel: 020 7953 3020, www.keytel.co.uk.

Sidi Saler €€€€ *Playa del Saler (12km/7 1/2 miles from Valencia), tel: 96 161 11 86, www.sidisaler.com.* Luxurious beach-side hotel in which all the rooms have a terrace and a sea view. Facilities include indoor and outdoor swimming pools, tennis and squash courts and a 'beauty farm'. For dining, there is both a formal restaurant and a brasserie offering a buffet. The hotel provides a minibus service for access to the city. 276 rooms.

DENIA

Buenavista €€€ *Tossalet 82, tel: 96 578 79 95, www.buenavistadenia.com.* Just outside the resort of Denia, this small hotel makes a relaxing base from which to explore the Costa Blanca. It stands in a wooded estate surrounded by a garden of aromatic Mediterranean plants and overlooks El Montgó natural park. There is a restaurant, swimming pool, sauna and gym. 17 rooms.

GANDIA

Molí el Canyisset €€€ *Carretera Font d'Encarros–Beniarjo, tel: 96 283 32 17, www.hotelcanyisset.es.* A rebuilt 17th-century rice mill, still distinguished by a tall brick chimney, 5km (3 miles) from Gandía's beaches. The rooms are spacious and stylishly decorated with a selection of antique and modern furniture. It has a restaurant, a massage room and a swimming pool. 16 rooms.

XATIVA

Huerto de la Virgen de Las Nieves €€–€€€ *Avenida de la Murta 10, tel: 96 228 70 58, www.huertodelavirgendelasnieves.com.* A 19th-century house which was built to preside over an orange grove outside the city walls. It has been carefully renovated and traditionally decorated with both new fittings and period furniture. The restaurant serves the two typical desserts of Xàtiva, *almoixávena* and *arnadi*. 8 rooms.

Mont Sant €€€ *Subida al Castillo, tel: 96 227 50 81, www.montsant.com.* A country house built on the ruins of a monastery at the foot of Xàtiva's castle, of which it has good views. It is surrounded by beautiful landscaped gardens. The rooms on the top floor of the main building have excellent views of Xàtiva. 17 rooms.

PENISCOLA

Hotel Agora €€–€€€ *Calle Huerto 80, tel: 902 88 63 86 www.hotelagorapeniscola.com.* A spacious and ultramodern hotel in the La Cantera area of Peñiscola, only 50 metres from the sea and not far from the historic quarter. Bedrooms are spacious with plenty of natural light, and well insulated. There are several swimming pools and a spa.

Parador de Benicarlo €€€ *Avenida Papa Luna 5, tel: 96 447 01 00, www.parador.es.* A parador beside the sea with a large garden and a swimming pool. It's located about 8km (5 miles) along the coast from Peñiscola. 108 rooms.

INDEX

Berlitz pocket guide

Valencia

Third Edition 2011

Written by Nick Inman and Clara Villanueva
Edited by Paula Soper and Siân Lezard
Series Editor: Tom Stainer

Photography credits
All Pictures APA Gregory Wrona except:
AKG London 15,17
Archivio Iconographico 18
APA Connor Caffrey 50
Felix Candela 5BM
Corbis 21, 22
Istockphoto 4/5, 4BL, 4BM, 4TL, 4TR, 5BR, 5TL, 5TR

Cover photograph: 4Corners Images

Every effort has been made to provide accurate information in this publication, but changes are inevitable. The publisher cannot be responsible for any resulting loss, inconvenience or injury.

Contact us

At Berlitz we strive to keep our guides as accurate and up to date as possible, but if you find anything that has changed, or if you have any suggestions on ways to improve this guide, then we would be delighted to hear from you.

Berlitz Publishing, PO Box 7910, London SE1 1WE, England.
email: berlitz@apaguide.co.uk
www.berlitzpublishing.com